Praise for **it's Not y**

"Laura Connell has written a must-read f̶̶̶̶̶̶̶̶̶̶̶̶ ̶̶̶̶̶̶̶ suffered at the hands of a toxic family. *It's Not Your Fault* brings together critical elements desperately needed for overcoming childhood shame, resulting addictions, and low self-esteem. Each chapter offers profound insight into some of the most common struggles faced by adult survivors."

DR. SHERRIE CAMPBELL, clinical psychologist and author of *Adult Survivors of Toxic Family Members*

"There are millions of people out there who don't realize that what keeps them in the vicious cycle of self-sabotage is the impact of growing up in a dysfunctional family. *It's Not Your Fault* is a powerful book of knowledge and wisdom for those whose invisible childhood wounds are preventing them from living their best life. Coupling personal experience with scientific research, Laura does a beautiful job of explaining 'the problem' in an extremely digestible way. She gives the reader great hope by outlining a path to healing that is both tangible and achievable. This is a must-read for anyone who grew up in a dysfunctional family system . . . so, basically, everyone!"

ANDREA ASHLEY, host of the *Adult Child* podcast

"Laura's book is a treasure chest of deep wisdom, empathy, and healing. For anyone that has put their life and dreams on hold as a result of living in a dysfunctional family; this book is for you. *It's Not Your Fault* not only shows how to recognize and heal from trauma, but also how to reconnect to life again, ignite your inner light, give strength to your inner voice, and step back into the world as the treasure you were born to be."

YASMIN KERKEZ, family relationship coach and co-founder of *Family Support Resources*

"Going through the pages of this book is a healing salve for anyone on a journey to find who they truly are after growing up in a dysfunctional environment. In *It's Not Your Fault*, Laura Connell offers a clear and innovative blueprint to help the reader dissolve the hurt that keeps them in self-abandonment, reclaim healthy love, and embody their authenticity when they no longer abide by the expectations that were projected onto them in dysfunctional dynamics."

XAVIER DAGBA, transformational coach and
shadow integration facilitator

"With compassion and clarity, Laura has written a breathtaking guidebook on identifying and healing self-sabotage. *It's Not Your Fault* is a shame-lifting read that will invite you you to meet yourself with the utmost care."

ASHLEY BEAUDIN, self-sabotage and
gentle business coach

"As a childhood trauma survivor, I wish I had read this book at the beginning of my healing journey. It is a powerful resource covering all aspects of trauma and recovery, and compassionately delivers practical tips for starting to heal yourself. As a trauma-informed coach, I highly recommend reading this book to anyone who wants to embark on a journey of self-discovery and recovery."

MARISA SIM, trauma-informed life coach

it's Not
your fault

it's Not your fault

THE SUBCONSCIOUS REASONS WE SELF-SABOTAGE AND HOW TO STOP

LAURA K. CONNELL

Health Communications, Inc.
Boca Raton, Florida

www.hcibooks.com

Library of Congress Cataloging-in-Publication Data
is available through the Library of Congress

ISBN-13: 978-07573-2473-4 (Paperback)
ISBN-10: 07573-2473-8 (Paperback)
ISBN-13: 978-07573-2474-1 (ePub)
ISBN-10: 07573-2474-6 (ePub)

Publisher: Health Communications, Inc.
        301 Crawford Boulevard, Suite 200
        Boca Raton, FL 33432–3762

Cover and interior design and formatting by Larissa Hise Henoch

This book is for you,
so you know you're not alone.

"One day you will tell the story
of how you overcame what you went through and
it will be someone else's survival guide."

BRENÉ BROWN

CONTENTS

ACKNOWLEDGMENTS

I WOULD LIKE TO THANK my agent Leticia Gomez of Savvy Literary; my editor at HCI, Christine Belleris; writing coach, Ann Kroeker; transformational life coach, Xavier Dagba; Writing Day Workshops; and hope*writers for their guidance in the art of writing and the business of publishing.

PREFACE

DO YOU BLAME YOURSELF for failing to reach your full potential in life, assuming it must be due to laziness, lack of willpower, or some other weakness on your part? Do you struggle with self-discipline and following through on all the things you want to do? Have you watched other people with fewer skills and credentials succeed, and wondered why you can't achieve the same goals even though you're smarter and more talented than they are? You can't help feeling you hold yourself back but struggle to understand why. And it's embarrassing because you're convinced other people are wondering the same thing about you.

In spite of your wonderful qualities, you feel undervalued and unappreciated, as though your needs don't matter. No matter how hard you try, you can't seem to get those needs met, and, if you're honest, you have trouble knowing exactly what it is you want anyway. Often, your thinking is muddled, and you walk around in a fog unable to see more than a few steps in front of you. It's a feat to get through the day, never mind formulating a plan on how to move forward in life. You spend most of your time reacting and surviving rather than creating a life you love.

The structure and routine that others put in place to help them reach their goals and organize their lives eludes you. Even when you manage to escape the chaos and implement some order, the rote repetition of daily tasks feels crushingly boring. You don't trust that consistency reaps reward because you've never seen it happen. So, you give up before you reach your goals and then chastise yourself for your weakness. Your inner critic runs the show no matter how many positive mantras you repeat to yourself because deep down you believe your critic is right.

Even though it's maladaptive, your habit of getting in your own way is designed to protect you against the disappointment and rejection that felt like life or death when you were a child. For example, rather than following through on a project and risk failure, you feel compelled to abandon your goal. If you don't finish, your subconscious mind reasons, no one can say you failed. This habit of abandoning yourself and what matters to you is called self-sabotage and it's the reason you feel like you never get what you want.

If self-sabotage sounds familiar to you, this book will help you navigate your way to healing. You'll show up for yourself in ways that build confidence and help you get the love, kindness, and respect you've always craved. You'll develop rock-solid routines that motivate you to follow through on all your plans. You'll lose the brain fog and gain clarity on who you are, what you want, your core values, likes, and dislikes.

I know because I've been where you are, spinning my wheels, falling short of my potential, and beating myself up about it every day. After studying the dynamics of dysfunctional families, I recognized unmet childhood needs as the source of my self-sabotage and unfulfilled dreams. I learned the secret to self-compassion and setting boundaries, and now I have a life where I'm on my own side instead of in my own way. I believe the same transformation is available to you and this book will provide you with the tools and knowledge to access it.

INTRODUCTION

"Find out who you are and do it on purpose."
DOLLY PARTON

I grew up in a dysfunctional family system with emotional abuse and neglect where I learned to stay small, even invisible, and put others' needs ahead of my own. As a result, I felt uncomfortable in my own skin, like there was something wrong with me, a fatal flaw. In high school, I discovered the power of alcohol to heal my feelings of discomfort and deficiency. My best friend gave me my first drink in her basement bar where her parents kept off-brand Bits and Bites alongside various bottles of alcohol. The first one-to-one concoction of orange juice and vodka replaced my isolation, discomfort, and shame with blissful oblivion. Suddenly, I said all the right things, met all the right people, and could show my feelings—and have them reciprocated.

I chased that feeling and looked forward to my next drink every day after that. As you can imagine, that dependence on alcohol led to a full-blown addiction in adulthood. Rather than drinking daily, I binged on weekends and suffered debilitating hangovers, along with regret from what I did and said the night before. After every drinking episode there were consequences I chose to ignore. My addiction worsened when I married someone who confirmed my belief there was something wrong with me. Near the end of our marriage, he would ask the accusatory question, "What's wrong with you?" I now know a more helpful query would have been, "What happened to you?"

His criticism and emotional neglect felt like home to me, and I stayed married to him for more than ten years. When the marriage ended, I began a journey away from self-abandonment and, less than a year later, faced my alcoholism and entered a recovery program. I learned that alcohol abuse is more than drinking, and recovery is about getting honest and digging deep to understand yourself and acknowledge how your past impacts your behavior.

This has meant curbing my relentless *doing* and taking time to examine and know myself as a human *being*. The most important piece of this puzzle has been learning to rely on God for my affirmation and validation rather than others. Slowly, I learned to stop putting myself last and fight for my life because no one else was going to. I stopped trying to please family members who would only shame me, and I learned to distance myself from them instead.

I studied the dynamics of dysfunctional families and realized how mine and the one I married into would do anything to resist changing their unhealthy habits. That's because toxic family systems are sustained by everyone staying in their roles. The one who has the courage and creative spirit to envision change is often scapegoated. The family would rather destroy the scapegoat than face the possibility that something needs to change.

It wasn't until my thirties that I learned how to implement healthy boundaries, in my recovery program. Before that, I never felt entitled to say "no" to anyone. Now that I'm over fifty, I've learned to set limits to protect myself and stop saying "sorry" for things that aren't my fault. The most important thing I've discovered is that others' negative reactions to your boundaries is proof they are working, not a cue to take them down. Those people are the reason you need boundaries in the first place.

It's not selfish to set boundaries or eliminate toxic people from your life, even if they're your family. It might be the hardest thing you've ever done—but you're worth it. You'll find you get better the more you practice saying no, setting limits, and taking time for yourself. And you have to receive grace when you don't do it perfectly. It's hard work to look within to discover the hidden obstacles to living a life you love. They can't be smoothed over by new habits or self-help mantras. They must be acknowledged, addressed, and challenged.

I had to investigate my past and how that impacted my behavior. My failure to stick with projects and so sabotage my own success had little to do with self-discipline and willpower. As you'll see, it had everything to do with being conditioned to give up when my mother failed to take care of my emotional needs as an infant. That's how far back this stuff can go.

And that's how this book differs from many other resources out there on the subject. If there's one thing I've learned from decades of therapy and self-exploration, it's that behavior modification doesn't work for everyone. Simply doing things differently while remaining the same inside might help for the short term, but it's exhausting. The minute you rest from the relentless task of positive self-talk and "good vibes," you fall right back into old patterns.

Once you decide to get serious about change and stop adjusting habits in the hope it will result in lasting transformation, you'll begin living a life not by reaction but by design. It takes a tremendous amount of work, an internal excavation, and that's why most people don't do it. They want the quick fix and seven simple steps, and they're disappointed when they never get where they want to be. But if you're ready to do the work, you can create the life you desire, and, if you're like me, it's nothing fancy. You want an intentional life, a life you love that includes you in the list of people you serve. What would that feel like?

CHAPTER ONE

BLIND SPOTS

"It is often the most spiritually healthy and advanced among us who are called on to suffer in ways more agonizing than anything experienced by the more ordinary."

M. SCOTT PECK

IN THE INTRODUCTION, I mentioned I was conditioned to give up in the face of challenges. That conditioning began as early as infancy when my mother neglected to meet my emotional needs. In *The Body Keeps the Score*, author Bessel van der Kolk affirms that if you've been abused or neglected, you learn that nothing you do or say will bring the help you need. This conditions you to give up when faced with challenges later in life.

The psychiatrist goes on to say that if your caregivers ignore your needs or appear to resent your existence, you learn to anticipate rejection and emotional withdrawal. Pete Walker, author of *Complex PTSD*, refers to "negative noticing," when children witness disdain instead of pleasure on their parents' faces. If you're like me, you've found it hard to relate to advice books that tell you all you need to do is think differently, adopt certain habits, or take a series of steps to get the results that have eluded you. You desperately want to believe success is that easy, and tweaking your habits may have worked for a while . . . but you always come back to your set point of self-sabotage.

For people from a supportive background and loving family, challenges feel good, like a normal part of the discomfort you must endure to move forward in life. They are not looking out for threats or wondering whether their needs will be met. They are relaxed and in a primed state to learn and take on challenges. For those of us who had a less-than-ideal journey to today, that same challenge feels like the rock of Sisyphus. The weight is so heavy we're sure it will crush us, and that's why we give up more easily.

In other words, it's not your fault. The traumatized brain does not want to play and explore or see where things go. It wants concrete answers, it wants to get things over with, and it does not want to make mistakes. Psychologist Jacob Ham calls this *survival brain versus learning brain.* He says "learning brain" is open to new information, comfortable with ambiguity, and sees the big picture. People with learning brain feel calm, peaceful, excited, playful, and curious about what they're going to learn. They're not concerned about making mistakes because they know that's part of the learning process. In fact, they're not really thinking about themselves at all and feel confident they'll apply themselves well enough to understand what they're about to learn.

People with "survival brain," on the other hand, are hyper-focused on threat. They can't tolerate ambiguity, want clear answers, and think in black-and-white terms. Survival brain makes people feel panicky, obsessive, and afraid of getting things wrong. As a result, they do not feel calm and open to learning new things and want to end the ordeal as quickly as possible. They are afraid of looking stupid if they make a mistake and are filled with self-doubt about their own ability to understand new concepts.

Dr. Ham's explanation helped me understand why I never felt safe unless I controlled every outcome. It explained why I had trouble accessing my playful side and why exploration and uncertainty produced unbearable stress instead of curiosity in me. It told me why I found it so hard to tolerate works in progress and could never relax until all the loose ends were tied up. It showed me why I was such a stickler for doing things the "right" way with no room for ambiguity or gray areas. My need to be right had cost me dearly in relationships and caused a rift with my adult children that lasted months.

If you've read books or articles on why you give up easily, you may have learned some version of "You're weak, you lack discipline," or "You need to believe in yourself more." What Dr. Ham shows us is that it's likely you're stronger than most. It's just that all your resources have gone into survival and there's little left over for less life-threatening challenges. Based on the household stressors you may have endured in childhood, many people we consider successful would wither in the face of what you've had to go through.

Even if your home was safe, your parents may have never encouraged you to persevere in the face of challenges. They let you quit whenever you wanted, so you learned if you don't like something you can stop doing it. You, my friend, have also been conditioned to give up easily. While it's sometimes wise to drop things we don't enjoy, it's also important to fulfill commitments and push through the unpleasant middle to obtain the end reward.

If you were raised without routines, it might be hard to understand how important they are to your success. You might wonder what's the point of making the bed when I'm only going to get in it again, or rail against the crushing boredom of standing at the kitchen counter preparing lunch for the next day. Such blind spots hold us back in ways our conscious minds find difficult to comprehend. I used to judge my work colleagues who packed lunch every day as dull drones. In reality, they were probably emulating the success-making habits of their attentive parents.

In addition to my haphazard eating schedule, I used to stay up until two or three in the morning, making me chronically tired and sleep-deprived the next day. This form of self-sabotage continued until my healing journey began in my late thirties. I never understood why I couldn't go to sleep at a normal time like other people and berated myself for repeating the same harmful pattern night after night. Now I know lack of encouragement from your parents can make it harder to switch off at night. Since you rarely received the pat on the back to indicate a job well done, you feel like you're never finished and there's more you could be doing (even if you're not doing it).

Do you resist going to bed at a reasonable hour even when you're tired? Cue the self-sabotage of late-night Netflix bingeing, Internet scrolling, and insufficient sleep. By implementing the tools you'll learn in this book, you can reassure your inner child she's done well today. You'll give yourself permission to "power down" for the night and feel satisfied you've *done* enough and you *are* enough.

Perhaps, instead, you grew up in a home where one or more parents ruled like a tyrant. Unlike the child without rules, you could barely breathe without being told to do so. It would seem logical that routine would come easier to you. But since you were pummeled with rules that made no sense, that's not the case. You're more likely to rebel against structure once you go out on your own because rules only served to oppress you in the past.

Both negligent and tyrannical parenting styles fail to help children develop the disciplines essential to success. As a result, the child grows up without realizing the importance of mundane tasks to overall life satisfaction and may not take steps to cultivate them. If you grew up in such a family, where no one taught you to establish *healthy* routines, developing them becomes an effective way to nurture yourself. They comfort by providing a rhythm you can count on.

Parents in healthy families teach their children the value of routines so they become ingrained in them and help them succeed in life. Because much of what paves the road to success is mundane, repetitive stuff, consistency is important—and it can be boring. But it's how we keep promises to ourselves and show ourselves we're worth the effort. Shifting your mindset to one that views routine as nurturing your inner child rather than mindless tedium will create lasting change and progress toward your goals. You'll no longer be held back or ruled by your temptations, and you'll stop making decisions based on how you feel in the moment.

Caring for yourself like a good parent means encouraging yourself to stay consistent even when it doesn't feel good. We sometimes have to do the opposite of what we feel when developing routines. That's not the same as being mean to yourself but a way of taking care of yourself to ensure long-term success and growth. When we say no to things that are bad for us, we gain strength and become a force for good in the world.

Routines like eating and sleeping at the same times bring comfort through their reliability. They reduce the number of decisions you have to make during the day. Decision fatigue is real and increases with each new decision you have to make, and studies show that as the day goes on, we make more impulsive decisions. When you know ahead of time what to expect (by having a sleeping and eating schedule, for example) you have one less thing to decide on. Without the routines in place that help us know when things are going to happen, we put ourselves in the position of making rash decisions at times when it is in our worst interest to do so.

Those times include later in the day (since decision fatigue gets worse as the day goes on) and when we're hungry (say, planning what to make for dinner). Decision-making in the moment leads to poor decisions or no decision at all. This, in turn, leads to disappointment in ourselves as we perpetuate the cycle of letting ourselves down. Simple, "boring" routines will help reduce the number of choices you have to make throughout the day. No more exhaustion from decision fatigue and you can spend that energy moving toward your goals.

Here are some areas to consider incorporating healthy routines in your life:

Focus on fitness: Moving your body for thirty minutes or so a day releases feel-good chemicals and sets you up for future health and a longer, better-quality life. It can give you clarity on issues that plague your mind and provide a balm for overthinking. If you've ever gone for a walk and experienced relief from the hamster wheel of thoughts in your head, you know what I mean. There's evidence walking can have a positive impact on trauma responses by alternately stimulating your right and left brain in the same way eye movement desensitization and reprocessing (EMDR) treatments work to relieve trauma in the body.

Minimize device time: Rather than looking at your phone several times throughout the day, set aside certain times to check e-mail and social media. For example, I check my e-mail in the morning, midday, and again in the evening and, for social media, once or twice a day. Decide how much time you want to devote to social media per day, then divide that time between your platforms and set your timer accordingly. Allowing yourself to react to every ping that comes through takes a toll on your nervous system, which increases anxiety, and prevents the focus needed to complete tasks.

Maintain a healthy diet: Eating wholesome meals at the same time every day will add years to your life. Preparing meals might feel boring at first but is an important form of self-care. Taking time to do meal prep on the weekend can pay dividends during the week when you're more likely to give in and order fast food. If you work away from home, taking a few minutes to pack your lunch the night before will increase your financial as well as physical health because take-out meals are high in both dollars and empty calories. Keeping these promises to yourself will increase your self-worth, which, in turn, will decrease your tendency to self-sabotage.

Don't (always) trust your feelings: Caring for yourself like a good parent means encouraging yourself to stick to a routine even when it doesn't feel good. We sometimes have to do the opposite of what we feel when developing healthy routines. For example, do you tend to isolate when you're feeling down? That's when it's time to pick up the phone and call someone, even when it might be the last thing you want to do. The trick is to make sure it's someone you trust with your feelings, not someone who will make you feel more misunderstood and alone. If you don't currently have someone like that in your life, you may want to seek out the help of a coach or counselor.

Be kind to yourself: If you grew up in a toxic family, it's especially easy to fall into the trap of chastising yourself when you don't do things perfectly. As you learn to develop healthy routines, forgive yourself when you slip or fall into old habits. Sometimes, you can glean good information from these so-called failures. We'll talk more about this later in Chapter 6.

Journal: It can help to take a written inventory at the end of each day and even throughout the day. What happened before you back-slid that triggered you? Write it down and see if you can find patterns. Encourage yourself to try again, reward yourself for progress not perfection, and congratulate yourself for having the courage to change. It takes more than behavior modification or following a few steps to overcome a lifetime of imprinting. Obstacles to success are often subconscious blind spots and the first key is to acknowledge these true barriers to getting what you want.

CHAPTER TWO

ATTACHMENT STYLES

"A securely attached child will store an
internal working model of a responsive,
loving, reliable caregiver, and of a self that
is worthy of love and attention and will
bring these assumptions to bear on
all other relationships."

JOHN BOWLBY

ONE OF THE SUBCONSCIOUS BARRIERS to getting what you want, especially in relationships, is your attachment style. Psychoanalyst John Bowlby developed the theory of attachment to help explain why infants became so distressed when separated from their parents. Bowlby confirmed these responses as normal because of the child's total dependence on the parent or caregiver for its very survival. As long as the caregiver is nearby, the child feels confident to branch out to play and explore and will return intermittently to the safety of the caregiver. If the caregiver is not near, the child experiences none of this confidence and freedom to wander and play and remains in a state of distress.

It's important to note the necessary nearness for the child to feel safe is not only physical but psychological. In fact, the psychological component is most important. If the parent is physically available but ignores the child's needs, the child will feel unsafe and insecure. Instead of sociable and relaxed, the child will feel anxious and preoccupied with searching for the parent or keeping herself safe.

Bowlby's colleague Mary Ainsworth performed an experiment that separated babies from mothers for a short time. They came up with three main categories of attachment based on how babies responded to their mothers leaving and then being reunited with them. Babies who were upset at the parent leaving but were easily comforted upon their return were labeled "secure." Babies who became extremely distressed when parents left and were not easily comforted when parents came back were labeled "anxious." Those who didn't seem distressed when parents left and who actively avoided contact once the parent returned were labeled "avoidant."

Secure Attachment

About 60 percent of babies were secure in their attachment and the responses of the babies correlated to relationship patterns in the home. The secure children had parents who were responsive to their needs. The anxious and avoidant children had parents who didn't respond to their needs or were inconsistent in their care.

Unfortunately for some of us, what happened in the past doesn't stay in the past. Attachment follows us into adulthood and affects the way we relate to others and the world. This will have a dramatic impact on our relationships. It's common sense that people with secure attachment would feel confident that their partner will meet their needs. They find it easy to depend on others and be there for others when needed.

These lucky people will tend to seek out others who share their secure attachment. If they meet someone who is emotionally cut off, they won't clamor to try to win their love. These people feel inherently deserving of love and affection because they received it from their parents or caregivers. Securely attached people have been gifted with skills from the previous generation on how to navigate relationships collaboratively rather than combatively.

If someone turns on them with rage or accuses them, they won't tolerate it because it doesn't feel right to them. They will be more adept at seeing those "red flags" and avoid getting too involved with someone who demonstrates these qualities. It's no surprise these types report enjoying longer-term and more trusting relationships. They've been primed since infancy to do so. These people have higher self-esteem and seek out social connections rather than preferring to be alone.

It stands to reason they will not devote a lot of time to relationships that are not healthy or beneficial to their well-being. This would not feel like "home" to them. Securely attached people believe love is enduring and they are worthy of it. It does not feel elusive or smothering. As a result, women with secure attachment report feeling happier with their romantic relationships than women with insecure attachments.

It's easy to see how difficulty in relationships can be attributed to attachment "style." If you were not aware of your attachment style, how could you have prevented it from sabotaging your relationships? Many of us have trouble understanding why our relationships have failed. It turns out the actions of our caregivers when we were infants had much to do with our inability to relate to others. How could we be blamed for something that altered us when we were still in the cradle?

A simple way to determine your attachment style is by choosing a paragraph below that you most closely relate to:

1. I am somewhat uncomfortable being close to others; I find it difficult to trust them completely, difficult to allow myself to depend on them. I am nervous when anyone gets too close, and often, others want me to be more intimate than I feel comfortable being.

2. I find it relatively easy to get close to others and am comfortable depending on them and having them depend on me. I don't worry about being abandoned or about someone getting too close to me.

3. I find that others are reluctant to get as close as I would like. I often worry that my partner doesn't really love me or won't want to stay with me. I want to get very close to my partner, and this sometimes scares people away.

If you answered 1, you display characteristics of an avoidant attachment style; 2 correlates to secure attachment; and 3 denotes an anxious attachment style. Because we gravitate to relationships that look like those with our primary caregivers, we have adopted a set of beliefs around what to expect from people and from the world. So, if we expect not to have our needs met, we'll seek out people who meet that expectation. If you're lucky enough to be securely attached, you'll gravitate to partners who are willing to take care of your needs and be interdependent with you. Some hallmarks of a securely attached person:

- Comfortable in a warm loving relationship
- Able to depend on others and have others depend on them
- Does not take a partner's or friend's need for space personally, and enjoys closeness
- Trusting, empathetic, forgiving, and tolerant of differences; shares feelings easily
- Communicates openly and honestly about emotions and does not avoid conflict
- Responsive to partner's or friend's needs
- Good emotional regulation; does not get upset easily over relationship issues
- Wants to resolve and forgive past issues and learn from them

In the following sections, we'll take an in-depth look at *insecure* attachment styles. These include the anxious and avoidant styles already mentioned and a third, less common, insecure style that impacts about 5 percent of the population. This style, called *disorganized* or *fearful avoidant*, displays both anxious and avoidant traits and results when fear has been the primary feeling toward the caregiver. This happens in cases where parents have suffered addictions and/or inflicted severe forms of abuse and neglect.

Anxious Attachment

A friend of mine began referring to the man she had been dating a few weeks as "the love of her life." By that time, she had already started taking care of his toddler daughter while he spent time with other people. When he ended their brief relationship after less than three months, she had to take two personal days off work to recover from her devastation. Many would question bestowing someone with "forever" status at such an early stage, not to mention babysitting his young child while he went off to play with his friends. To my friend, however, that behavior was part of a recurring relationship pattern.

Anxiously attached people will report falling in love over and over rather than sustaining one long-term love relationship. They need constant affirmation that they are loved and cared for. Their neediness feels suffocating to others and pushes them away, repeating the destructive cycle and making them feel as though their needs are unmet yet again. This results in frequent breakups, which leave them almost inconsolable. They are often terrified of being alone even for short times and have an insatiable need for closeness and intimacy. They might get labeled as overly emotional.

Anxious attachment will make someone feel insecure in their relationship and they will be quickly frustrated if needs are not met. They appear clingy and needy and end up repelling their partners, the opposite of their heart's desire. Here are the hallmarks of anxious attachment style:

- Insecure in relationships and constantly worried about being rejected or abandoned

- Needs constant reassurance and wants to merge with partner, which scares the person away

- Low self-esteem but thinks highly of others

- Obsesses over relationship issues and appears clingy and desperate

- Overly sensitive to partner's actions and moods and takes their behavior personally

- Highly emotional and argumentative, controlling, and has poor boundaries

- Stirs up conflict rather than communicating in a healthy way

Anxious attachment is one outcome of inconsistent parenting. The child never knows whether the parent will be supportive or unavailable, so she becomes confused about the relationship and never knows what to expect. Another reason for anxious attachment is the parent using the child to fulfill her own need for emotional contentment rather than seeking to be there for the child. She appears to be overprotective but uses the child to increase her own image as an ideal parent. Separation in early childhood from a parent or caregiver can also contribute to development of an anxious attachment style, say, if the mother became sick and had to spend time in the hospital.

Unlike the avoidant, an anxiously attached person is highly dependent on others and needs the presence of a loved one to feel okay. She can rarely relax because of the constant worry of abandonment. Though she is sensitive and in tune with her partner's emotional needs, she often gravitates to avoidant partners. When this person fails to meet her needs, she'll blame herself and take it as proof of her unworthiness.

She might make up a fantasy of a stable relationship and ignore all indications that things aren't right and then get blindsided when the relationship ends despite all the warning signs. Even if someone all but ignores her, she believes he is the one who will solve all her problems. She believes he will make her life perfect if only she can uncover the "real" him. She believes that once he sees the light, he will understand they were meant for each other, and she can finally feel complete.

As in childhood, she may carry the erroneous belief that if she gives more and needs less, she will win him over. Unlike the avoidant who asserts her independence in a relationship, the anxious person will give up all her needs to take care of the other person's desires. Her constant fear of abandonment results in jealousy, clinginess, and an inability to simply enjoy her partner's company, explore, and grow in the relationship.

If you see yourself or someone you love in this description, there is hope. Sometimes, change will happen as a result of being in relationship with a securely attached person. They will show you love and emotional closeness and provide the security you require in a relationship.

Whether or not you find such a partner, you will likely need to do some work. Pay attention to how you interact with your relationship partner and your emotions as they come up in response to feeling insecure in the relationship.

Talk to others besides your partner about your feelings. Whether a friend, family member, or therapist, practice relying on people other than your partner to help you regulate your emotions. Notice when you are talking at someone rather than connecting with them in conversation. Connection is a two-way street and if you talk to someone you should give them a chance to reciprocate.

Otherwise, they will see you as caring only about your own needs. This will cause them to pull away, further harming your sense of security.

Forgive yourself for the ways you learned to cope when your parents weren't there for you. You kept yourself safe by controlling and worrying when your needs went unmet as a child. But now you can let go of those coping mechanisms and find healthier ways to express your needs. Seek out securely attached partners and be open and honest about what you need. Let them know if you want them to check in with you and that separation is hard for you, so you need to know when you'll come together again.

By the same token, let go of relationships with insecurely attached people as this will only exacerbate your pain and make growth difficult, if not impossible. Although the prospect of being alone can be terrifying, it's a pain that's worthwhile to face and overcome. When you face this fear, you'll find being alone less painful than being with someone who stirs up your insecurities and leaves you feeling anxious. You might decide to take a certain amount of time away from romantic relationships while you work on nurturing yourself.

Relationships are important to you and that's a good thing. However, it's necessary to have balance in your life by developing your own interests, friendships, and support groups outside your romantic partnership. Then when a relationship does come along, you won't be so quick to give up everything for another person. Develop self-validation rather than seek approval from outside sources. This means learning how to connect authentically with your feelings and needs, then finding ways to meet those needs yourself rather than relying on a partner to meet them for you.

Avoidant Attachment

When I became pregnant with my first child, my ex-husband responded with nonchalance. Rather than hug me or express delight, he made a comment about how he'd have to work harder now. When pregnancy hormones led me to ask him to hold me as a form of comfort, he refused. When the baby started kicking inside me, I invited him to put his hand on my stomach to feel it. He pulled away in revulsion and left the room shuddering, saying it felt weird, like an alien inside me.

Avoidant attachment is one outcome of a childhood in which closeness was dangerous because someone abandoned you or withdrew their love. This behavior has its roots as far back as infancy and even what happened in the womb. If a child was not wanted, if his emotional needs went unmet, or he was expected to care for himself too soon, he may have developed an avoidant attachment style. People with avoidant attachment tell themselves they don't need close relationships. They will not feel comfortable asking for and receiving help and will not want anyone being too dependent on them.

It's not a matter of whether his family was rich or poor, or whether his mother worked outside the home. Avoidant attachment style can form if the parent was present but did not allow the child to express his feelings fully. The more intense the emotions, the more disapproving the parent becomes. The child learns his emotions are not welcome and are not a source of bonding. In fact, they push people away. So, he may grow up to avoid emotions, suppress them, or detach from them.

This is why emotionally neglected children often grow up to feel unreal. If as a child you feel unseen or unheard, you can develop a poor sense of self and depersonalize, which means you feel as though you don't matter, that you don't really exist. Some have described it as looking at themselves from above or feeling weightless, or as though their surroundings are fuzzy and blurred. Can you imagine how difficult it would be to navigate your way through life when you don't even know who you are? Maybe you don't have to imagine.

It is the job of our caregivers to help us understand ourselves, to develop our strengths and weaknesses, and to guide us on this path through life. If that mentoring was lacking or nonexistent, it's no wonder we have trouble discerning what we're meant to do or even what we're good at. Emotional neglect can be as damaging as emotional abuse and wreak havoc on relationships, even though the cause of this style of relating is often unknown to the person who displays it.

It's easy to see how such a discomfort with emotional highs and lows and an intolerance of emotional expression will negatively impact relationships. That's why avoidant people struggle to develop long-lasting fulfilling relationships. Someone with avoidant attachment believes love is rare and temporary. They might think romantic love is a fairy tale and doesn't happen in real life.

Avoidant people have trouble expressing emotions or even voicing their thoughts in relationships, and this deprives them of intimacy. They invest little emotion in their social and romantic relationships and, for this reason, experience little distress when relationships end. They use excuses like work to avoid spending quality time with people and are likely to fantasize about others during sex. They are also more likely to engage in casual relationships and may even prefer them to long-term ones. They also have trouble supporting their partners through hard times.

Avoidants can be the most sociable people with lots of friends and connections. But try to talk about anything intimate and they often shut down. When you attempt to deepen the relationship, you will be rebuffed, and they will close the door on you. They seem nice, but they won't go any further than the surface with you and that's frustrating and confusing. At the point where you seek to increase closeness, they might become contemptuous or critical and look for ways to end the relationship.

Here are some hallmarks of avoidant attachment style:

- Creates emotional distance in relationships
- Avoids intimacy as this makes them feel a frightening loss of independence
- Resents having others depending on them, and struggles to depend on others or ask for help
- Avoids conflict—then explodes later
- Calm, cool, and collected; avoids feeling or talking about emotions
- Good in a crisis, nonemotional, takes charge
- Appears to have high self-esteem because he is self-sufficient and can do well in business

The caregiver deficiencies discussed above have led these people to turn off their need for emotional attachment. They have been primed to believe they do not need it and it is dangerous to rely on or trust other people. The saddest part is this is all subconscious, and the avoidant is likely suffering but has no idea how to get the closeness others enjoy.

If you see yourself or someone you love in this description, don't lose hope; attachment styles can change with some work. It is challenging and takes a tremendous amount of effort because you're going against a lifetime of conditioning. Start with looking at why you might cut people off easily. Do you sever ties over something trivial and move on quickly?

Do you marvel at how others sob and fret over losing a friend and think, *Why do they care so much?* Learning to allow people to make mistakes and not end relationships over inconsequential matters can be the first step to healing avoidant attachment. Try telling the person how you feel instead of keeping things bottled up inside. For example, if a friend has a habit of canceling plans at the last minute, tell her you'd appreciate more notice instead of stopping contact or refusing to take her calls. You may fear opening up will result in rejection and contempt. In a strange way, revealing a need feels life-threatening, which makes perfect sense since in childhood, abandonment could mean death. You may be surprised when your friend expresses remorse over canceling your plans last minute and agrees to give more notice in the future. Taking this small step of expressing yourself will help you realize that people are understanding if you give them the opportunity.

You can also reciprocate when friends share their troubles with you. Until now, you may have taken the listener role and never let yourself be vulnerable enough to share your feelings and struggles. There are two reasons for this: First, you believe sharing your struggles will make you a burden because you grew up in a home where your feelings were never validated, and your parents' needs came first; second, it feels too scary to let someone see your flaws. You fear revealing your weaknesses will compromise your need (developed in childhood to protect yourself in the face of neglect) to rely only on yourself.

If you take the chance to reveal yourself, you may see the fruits of your labor when people do not pull away when you share "weakness" but draw closer instead. They may even respect you more. Your opinion of people will change when you see the warm-hearted, loving natures many will display when given the chance to enter your emotional world. Before, you assumed people didn't care because you had never given them anything to care about. You may discover the reality is quite different. Most people are beautifully flawed and forgiving, and desire intimacy.

As you open up, you'll begin to enjoy the friendship of people who are securely attached and able to embrace a range of emotions. While you viewed your needs as a burden, they see mutual support as a natural part of friendship. You might find it beneficial to write in a journal about your true thoughts and feelings. Here are some prompts you can use:

Which emotion am I trying to avoid right now?

Why am I hiding from this emotion?

What is this emotion wanting to tell me?

These changes can feel frightening and won't happen overnight. In fact, it could take years, but you will see progress in the meantime that will help you celebrate and keep going. It's best to start small and work your way up to scarier self-revelation.

Disorganized Attachment

A fourth category, called disorganized attachment, arises when a parent is inconsistent and unreliable due to mental illness, addiction, or their own unresolved trauma. The child does not know which parent she will get from one moment to the next and therefore does not know whether the parent will be a source of comfort or terror. Here are some hallmarks of a disorganized attachment style:

- Haunted by memories of past trauma but has not resolved or mourned what happened
- Intolerant of emotional closeness, prone to rages, poor emotional regulation that can lead to abuse
- Suffers from PTSD from traumatic memories and their triggers
- Shuts down emotionally to cope with life, which can lead to depression
- Lack of empathy; possible narcissism, substance abuse, or borderline personality disorder
- Feels helpless and ineffective in life
- Has trouble setting and achieving goals
- Alternates between clinginess and detachment (displays attributes of both anxious and avoidant types)

Someone with disorganized attachment style suffers from elements of both the anxious and avoidant types. It is thought to result from abuse and other childhood trauma where the central factor in the child's upbringing has been fear. Disorganized attachment results when the main source of support (a parent or caregiver) is also a source of terror. The very person who is supposed to care for the child instills in that child a fear for her own safety. The child has no idea if or when her needs will be met, which creates a sense that the world is an unsafe place and others cannot be trusted.

Whereas the avoidant has a high opinion of self and low opinion of others, the anxious person has low self-esteem and holds others in high regard, the disorganized person has a low view of self, others, and the world at large. She is in a constant state of protecting herself against perceived threats. While the avoidant has given up looking to the caregiver for support and the anxious child is still seeking it, the disorganized child lacks any coherence in her approach to the caregiver. She seeks closeness while also recoiling in fear.

Adults with disorganized attachment desperately want intimacy but are terrified of getting hurt. Although they want closeness and love, they are afraid of what will happen if they let anyone in and project onto their partner that fear. They expect to get hurt and see this pain as inevitable as they have no reason to believe anyone will love and support them for who they are.

Sometimes, they will break up with someone to preempt the rejection they fear. Or they will act hot and cold with new partners, which frustrates and pushes them away and in turn only reinforces the fear that the person is unloved and unwanted.

If you see yourself or someone you love in this description, there is hope. Since the key fear of disorganized attachment is being hurt by someone you trust, you have simply decided not to trust anyone. Disorganized attachment is like trying to play the game of life without ever having learned the rules. You desperately desire a loving relationship but have no idea how to cultivate one.

Learning to trust people is the first step for someone with

disorganized attachment. This can be challenging, and it will help to seek the support of a therapist or counselor who makes you feel supported. This may not be the first one you see. But if this is too expensive or you're unable to trust a therapist at this time, the following are strategies you can use to heal on your own.

Start feeling the pain associated with your past experiences rather than locking those feelings away. When you bury pain, it doesn't go away but comes out sideways at inopportune times and can look like explosive rage that has nothing to do with the present moment. Without facing your past, you could be triggered at any moment and have little control over your reactions.

One of the key traits of disorganized attachment is an incoherent narrative surrounding one's childhood. It's important to begin to tell the truth about what happened to you and stop making excuses for your parents' behavior toward you. That is not the same as blaming them. You may wish to consider how their own childhoods left them ill-equipped to parent you adequately, not to excuse them but to make sense of their behavior toward you.

Creating a coherent narrative of your past will improve your self-image and help you feel more "real." It will also help you understand why you've behaved the way you have, and to forgive yourself because it's not your fault. The inner critic is especially harsh and self-loathing with disorganized attachment, so it's important to tell a different story about yourself, not with mantras, but with concrete examples from your life.

Since disorganized attachment shows up more in romantic relationships, think of positive things your friends or coworkers say about you. Make a list of your talents and good qualities and read them to yourself. Give yourself credit for doing the hard work of wanting to improve. Practice expressing your needs calmly and clearly. It makes sense that your communication skills would be underdeveloped if your caregivers ignored you or forbade you from asserting yourself.

Your confidence will grow as you reap the rewards of more open communication. You might even see how relationships can flourish when people talk to each other about their thoughts and feelings.

As with the anxious style, it's important to seek out securely attached people as partners. Avoidant types will set you off and confirm your worst fears. You may decide to take some time out from romantic relationships and dating while you work on healing your disorganized attachment style. As you "earn" a more secure attachment style, you will attract more securely attached people who will help you heal further and resolve your past trauma. It's important to note the road to healing will be long and arduous and change will not happen overnight.

You might find you make forward progress only to fall back when triggered. But it's the overall movement that matters. Remind yourself how you've changed when you compare how you've dealt with a present-day conflict with the past, then celebrate your incremental wins. Warning: life might feel dull without the constant chaos and disruption of your past relationships, at least temporarily. Remind yourself that you're building a new "home" unlike the old abusive one that you subconsciously drew toward and tried to emulate in your romantic relationships.

Emotional intensity is a positive quality and one you may want to channel into creative pursuits and other areas where you can fulfill that need for feeling and connection. A life without conflict is not the goal. Instead, you'll allow yourself to learn from those conflicts and view them as personal growth opportunities. No longer will they feel like painful missiles lobbed at you; instead they will become necessary steps on the path to understanding yourself. You'll find you won't have to keep repeating the same mistakes and patterns. You'll do things differently the next time even when you don't get it exactly right.

CHAPTER THREE

FAMILY SCAPEGOATING

"If you are silent about your pain,
they'll kill you and say you enjoyed it."

ZORA NEALE HURSTON

ONE OF MY CLIENTS, Sarah, came to me because she dealt with a bullying husband whom she felt had turned her children against her. Through our work together, I learned Sarah's mother had suffered with an undiagnosed mental illness, which made her incapable of experiencing empathy or compassion, two of the most important components of mother-child bonding. Sarah's role in the family involved taking on the burden of her mother's emotional neediness while displaying no needs of her own. Her basic material wants were covered but her emotional needs got ignored and discouraged. She came out of that household primed to put her needs last and to expect to be treated as if she existed to satisfy the needs of others.

As an adult, Sarah attracted a husband who insisted she give up a job where she felt happy and fulfilled and work for his company instead. When she asked for his support to ease an overwhelming workload, he accused her of stirring up trouble and seeking attention. Instead of taking her side when the children disrespected her, he encouraged them by saying she caused all the problems in the family. If it weren't for her, he said, they would all be happy.

Sarah felt confused and filled with self-doubt over her family's behavior toward her. She questioned whether they might be right, but something inside told her she was not who they made her out to be. Due to my understanding of these shaming tactics, I could see Sarah served as a convenient diversion from her family's real problems, which were multifaceted and generational. Because I'd studied the dynamics of dysfunctional family systems, I could easily discern her archetypal role as the repository for the family's grievances. They used her as the scapegoat for their own shortcomings, making her the problem instead of facing their own need to change.

The scapegoat is first mentioned in the Bible as a living sacrifice of a goat. Rather than kill the animal, the community releases the "scapegoat" into the wild to carry away with it the sins of the whole group. The group casts out the scapegoat and leaves it to its own devices. Its only purpose is to bear the burden of sins that are not its own. Today, we sometimes see scapegoats in governments and corporations as whistleblowers who suffer as a result of their decisions to expose corrupt practices. In this chapter we'll talk about scapegoats in dysfunctional families where one person gets singled out to take the blame for all the problems of the clan. Instead of looking at themselves, the family points a collective finger at the scapegoat. Rather than a conscious decision, the group subconsciously agrees to attack the one who threatens to expose the dynamics of the family system. This allows them to carry on in their dysfunctional patterns without changing. They pretend to themselves they're all right while the scapegoat is all wrong.

The scapegoat is the one who tells the truth about obvious defects in the family. Rather than support, the scapegoat experiences gaslighting from the rest of the family. That means your natural human reaction to the family's troubles or poor treatment of you becomes the focus instead of the issue itself. It is a form of psychological abuse in which the perpetrator denies or minimizes your experience. It's a cruel emotional manipulation that makes you doubt yourself and even reality.

I know how this feels. One Thanksgiving, for example, I arrived home after traveling for hours in stormy weather to discover my family had eaten without me. When I asked why they wouldn't wait after I'd made such an effort to get there, my sister crossed her arms over her chest and growled, *"Why do you always come in and make everybody feel like shit?"* Then they returned to their conversation as if I had never spoken. Her gaslighting shut me up and put me in the role of the bad guy when I was the one who had been wronged. Sadly, the tactic worked, and I believed the lie that stating my feelings made me an irreparably horrible person.

The family convinces the scapegoat that she is damaged, wrong, overreacting, and a liar. They make her question herself and even reality. She may be the mentally healthiest member of the family but by banding together, the clan convinces itself, and the scapegoat, that the opposite is true. She is often the most creative, sensitive, and honest family member who is more willing to see and speak the truth behind the facade of the family image. She may not understand why the rest of the family is unwilling to admit the obvious, keeps secrets, and hides the truth. For the scapegoat, the truth will set you free, but she is part of a family system that would rather remain in chains.

Fear of change and exposure motivates the family to sacrifice the scapegoat this way. Rather than face the truth and the possibility of deconstructing the whole family system, they demonize the truth teller. They may even influence people outside the family to mistrust her to further strengthen their case against her. If any of this resonates with you and you believe you've been targeted as the family scapegoat, here are nine signs that you and I have something in common. It may be hard to have your experience mirrored back to you, but I promise not to leave you here without hope. Before the chapter closes, I'll take you through a gentle six-point plan to find the healing and self-love to relieve your pain and heartache.

1. You are punished for telling the truth

It seems like anytime you speak the truth, your family rebukes you. They abandon or punish you when you don't go along with the status quo. They can't acknowledge the obvious truths you point out and instead point the finger at you and say you are the one with the problem. They may ignore or humiliate you to make you stay quiet because they won't risk entertaining the idea that what you say is true.

2. You are the whistleblower

Perhaps you threatened to expose a family secret but somehow got branded the bad guy. That's because your desire to bring the truth to light poses a threat to a family dynamic that functions in the dark by keeping secrets and protecting its public image instead of you. It's a system built like a house of cards, and they fear it will come toppling down if they believe you. The hardest part of being a scapegoat is that families can be exceptionally good at hiding their dysfunction. This results in further isolation when the victim is not believed.

3. Your family blames you for their shortcomings

They refuse to examine the poor behavior you're asking them to acknowledge. Instead, they point to your human reaction to that behavior and pretend that's the issue instead. What's happening is a cruel act of triggering someone to react, then punishing them for their reaction. A valid human response becomes further evidence the scapegoat is "crazy" or always stirring up trouble. In addition, if someone in the family does something wrong, they'll find a way to blame you for it instead.

4. You're held to a different standard

Other people get away with all kinds of terrible behavior, but when you step out of line just a little you feel the full force of the family's ire. You may notice thoughts and opinions similar to yours are celebrated when others express them, but when you say or do the same things you get maligned. In psychology, this is known as the "black sheep effect." Family members who deviate from the accepted "norm" are judged more harshly than those outside the family.

5. You feel left out

You may find yourself left out of family events or conversations. Because you tell the truth, they'd rather not hear from you. The last thing they want is your insight because that would force them to look at themselves and the ways they need to change. At the same time, you may get criticized for your absence at events you were never invited to. This provokes guilt in you even though you're the one who has been ostracized.

6. They sully your reputation

Family members talk about you behind your back and try to brainwash your few supporters against you. They speak poorly of you even to those outside the family circle. Rather than face their dysfunction they'll tarnish your reputation publicly. This is so you won't receive support from outside the family and they can continue in their collective delusion.

7. Your family makes you feel ashamed or guilty

As a result of years of unjust treatment, you have internalized a false sense of being bad or wrong. You have trouble standing up for yourself and accept too much blame. This can lead to over responsibility as you try to prove your "goodness." You blame yourself for negative outcomes over which you have little to no control, feeling overwhelmed with shame rather than merely disappointed. You might fail to protect yourself from offenses against you as a means of "taking the high road." You always have to be the bigger person and bear the burden of repairing relationships that are either bad for you or not your job to fix. You likely do this by allowing the other person to escape accountability for their poor treatment of you.

8. You receive little or no praise

Your family downplays your accomplishments. You may have never been praised or encouraged for your achievements in life. Without the motivation provided by a pat on the back for a job well done, you may give up and fail to achieve anything close to your potential. On the flip side, you may work ever harder trying to prove yourself. Since you haven't experienced the validation of a job well done, you'll never know when to stop, which leads to exhaustion and an inability to relax.

9. You have a difficult relationship with your sibling(s)

You have trouble connecting with your siblings as equals. They treat you with the same disdain as the rest of the family, promoting a false narrative of you as a troublemaker, or even someone with mental health issues. They treat you with disrespect and seem to discredit you at every turn. They do not provide you with the support you see in other sibling relationships. As mentioned, they do not celebrate your achievements with you but find ways to downplay them.

While there's no magic number that confirms you are a family scapegoat, it's safe to say answering yes to five or more of these signs would be a good indication. It's important to know it's not your fault and you have/had no control over your position within the family. It's a role that was forced on you from a young age. Being stuck in the role of the scapegoat impacts you long after you've grown and left the family home. It holds you back in all areas of your life through self-sabotage that you blame on yourself when you don't understand the root cause.

Obstacles to Success

In the 1950s, British pediatrician and psychoanalyst Donald Winnicott developed the concept of the "good enough mother." Children who grow up in healthy or "good enough" family systems, have parents and family members who have helped them discover who they are: their likes and dislikes, what they're good at and not so good at. Their parents observe these strengths and weaknesses and help them develop a plan for their lives. They guide them on a path to success, or at least a somewhat fulfilling life. Even when they don't get it right all the time, these parents want what's best for their child.

Winnicott observed that parents need not be perfect, and, in fact, children benefit when their parents fail from time to time. But that's only if they fail in ways the child can tolerate, not a consistent pattern of abuse and neglect. Not only did your parents not get it right (if you were the scapegoat), but they also committed grievous harm against you, whether consciously or subconsciously. They sacrificed you to prop up a nefarious family system. It's easy to see how a complete lack of encouragement coupled with a refusal to acknowledge or celebrate success would demotivate a child and lead to self-sabotage. It would de-incentivize that little one from taking risks or meeting challenges without any support system. It's not the child's fault he's been conditioned to give up as he's been taught that nothing he does will ever be good enough.

If you're the scapegoat, you've been primed to give up easily due to a lack of encouragement and devaluing of your achievements. Of course, this will impact your success in life as growth requires pushing forward in the face of challenges and receiving rewards along the way. As a result of scapegoating, you may accept jobs that don't use your strengths and abilities. You settle for roles you're overqualified for because you've been convinced you can't do any better or don't deserve more.

Despite having earned a degree from one of the top universities in the country, I spent most of my career working in low-paid administrative positions. Friends would encourage me to go for more but I could never fight the feeling that I didn't have what it took to strive for something better. I stayed below the radar, unable to shake the feeling that standing out equated with danger. After working with a trauma-informed life coach in my forties, I discovered this feeling started in toddlerhood when I sought my mother's attention as she talked on the phone. Without warning, she smacked me hard across the face. That incident imprinted me with the belief that visibility meant pain and abandonment. As a result, I missed opportunities to shine, show off my talents and abilities, and challenge myself to grow beyond my comfort level.

This mentality is in keeping with the conditioning of the scapegoat that she is fatally flawed, different from other people, and less than. You may experience workplace bullying and general disrespect from others. Standing up for yourself never got you anywhere in your family, so you conclude it's easier to stay quiet, avoid conflict, and fly under the radar. Such a passive approach to life makes you an easy target for abuse from bullies and being taken advantage of by more dominant types. You may allow colleagues to steal your ideas without challenging them. You may even tolerate illicit behavior such as harassment, whether in the form of jokes or innuendos designed to belittle you, or inappropriate physical touch.

Relationship Issues

Instead of helping you develop your sense of self, your family brainwashed you with a false narrative of who you are. Due to your family's betrayal, you find it difficult to trust people and form secure relationships. You may exhibit traits of the avoidant attachment style because you've learned to play your cards close to the vest. Revealing too much about yourself got you punished or discredited so you've learned to protect yourself by saying little about your thoughts, feelings, and opinions. This protective mechanism hurts you in relationships. You deprive yourself of intimacy when you're afraid to share the full spectrum of your inner life with someone else.

Even as an adult, when anything goes wrong in a relationship with a family member you are blamed. And you have probably internalized this blame. I know I did. Any tension between myself and my mother got framed as my fault. I accepted that blame and tried desperately to make things better. I sacrificed myself to keep the relationship, but it wasn't a true relationship because in a positive loving relationship, the needs of both parties are valued and discussed. Both sides take responsibility for their part in the rift, and both do their part to fix it.

Justifiably, you've internalized anger from a lifetime of absorbing so much negative attention. To deal with the terrible sense of unworthiness that's been inflicted on you, you may resort to substance abuse or other unhealthy coping mechanisms to deal with the trauma. Suppressing anger can also impact your health through stress-related disease, or make you feel on edge, depressed, or anxious. You may be dealing with a full-blown addiction and likely have issues with codependence. At its core, codependence means you rely on someone else's approval to feel whole. Codependent relationships are based on enabling, where one person tacitly supports another in their addiction, poor mental health, or failure to take responsibility.

How to Heal if You Are the Family Scapegoat

If the nine signs of scapegoating sound familiar to you, take heart. As promised, I will walk you through a path to healing that will help you find freedom from the lingering effects of family scapegoating. As mentioned, the scapegoat can be the mentally healthiest member of the family. Your qualities of honesty and sensitivity will now work in your favor as they help you heal from the trauma you've experienced. Here are six ways to reclaim your life from the lies your family has told you:

1. Create healthy boundaries

You may believe familial relationships should be kept at all cost. Whenever you shared your feelings about your family's treatment of you, the listener may have replied, "But, she's your mother," or something similar. But if your family has been abusing you, either physically or emotionally, you have the right to protect yourself. You can stand up and refuse to tolerate the abuse any longer.

I know what's it's like to be surprised by behavior that's been going on as long as you can remember. Unless someone has demonstrated a sincere desire to change, chances are they're not going to. Plan before a visit how you will react when the inevitable happens and your family member criticizes you or worse. If available, get support from another trusted individual before, during, and after one of these encounters, so you're not needing the person's approval. If you're inclined to spend the energy, ask the toxic person to clarify their meaning every time they offend you. Or warn them in advance of your parameters, for example, you will leave the room if they speak to you in a rude or critical manner.

This may still prove too stressful for you and make you feel exhausted after every interaction. If so, move to neutral ground. Instead of meeting in their home or yours (where you can't leave if you feel triggered), meet them in a coffee shop every few weeks or months and make small talk. If they try to engage in old patterns of criticizing and judging you, stay silent or steer the conversation back to surface level where you feel safe. After you've put in a predetermined amount of time, look at your watch and say it's time for you to go.

This might sound superficial and feel wrong, but it serves to protect you. Neither of you benefit when the conversation devolves, and you go back to your roles of abuser and abused. This method provides a stopgap measure while you decide whether to continue the relationship.

Instead of making a rash decision, give yourself time and space to come to a healthy conclusion. You decide, unhurried, whether you can tolerate this person in your life.

If the answer is no, you can make the difficult decision to cut ties. Stopping contact with people who hurt you is often a last resort and happens when you can't forge a functional relationship. If someone is physically dangerous or emotionally threatening, then you need to get away from them immediately, and enlist law enforcement or other support. If you feel depressed and physically sick after seeing this person, and they refuse to listen to your requests to be treated with respect, cutting ties might be the only reasonable option. Only you can make that decision and, if you do, it's crucial that you find support outside the family. To maintain the family system, your relatives might combine their efforts to bully and discredit you. They may even approach your close friends with lies about how they're worried about you and concerned over your mental health. This is called "mobbing" and can feel incredibly difficult to withstand on your own.

2. Let go of the longing for your family to accept you

Accept that nothing you do is likely to make your abusers acknowledge wrongdoing. No matter how reasonable and rational your position, they will not understand because they don't want to. They may never apologize for what they've done to you. More likely, they will double down on making you wrong. By keeping the focus on your supposed shortcomings, they deflect attention away from the real problem, which is their dysfunctional family dynamic. Instead of hoping for something you'll never receive, move forward, and forge a new identity based on the truth of who you are.

3. Change the narrative

You must challenge the story about yourself that your family has placed in your head. Look honestly at the situation and put some critical distance between yourself and them. Understand you've been punished disproportionately to anything you may have done. Most often, you are targeted simply for telling the truth! You are not bad or wrong or have a fatal flaw that makes you unlovable. To remind yourself of this, make a list of your good qualities and read it to yourself often. As you heal from the damaging effects of scapegoating, let God or your Higher Power provide you with the comfort you never received from family members. You are not who your parents or family say you are.

4. Practice self-care

This may feel difficult at first as you've likely internalized a punitive attitude toward yourself and have a loud inner critic. Set aside time each day to tune into what you want and provide it to yourself. You may have become detached from your most basic needs that start in the body. Perhaps you need to take a deep breath or have a cup of tea. Spend time each day doing something you enjoy, whether that's journaling, going for a walk, or getting yourself a treat. You may have trouble discerning your likes and dislikes but that will come gradually as you get to know yourself better. In Chapter 8, we'll go more in depth on how to connect with yourself this way.

Only take responsibility for your part. It's common for scapegoats to be and feel overly responsible in all relationships and this is how they try to earn their goodness. By taking more than their share of the blame, they feel like they are doing the right thing and being the bigger person. But this enabling behavior prevents others from taking responsibility for their part. It keeps you stuck in a role of absorbing blame for other people's problems or transgressions. That's no longer your role to play.

5. Lean on support

As you do the hard work of removing yourself from the scapegoat role in a toxic family, you'll need support. This could be a trauma-informed coach or counselor, support group, faith-based group, or trusted loved ones. Ensure these people understand your situation and empathize. People who don't understand can do further damage and set you back in your progress. Make sure you determine the trustworthiness of people before you share your struggles with them. Sometimes, in your need to feel understood, you can overshare with someone who has not earned the right to hear your story. Start with something small and see if they reciprocate. With those trustworthy people, practice sharing your authentic thoughts, feelings, and opinions with them.

You've been conditioned to keep quiet to avoid being punished or misunderstood. But that only hinders the intimacy and connection you crave. Practice opening slowly to one or two people. Share with them something you're feeling and see if they match your vulnerability. This is how loving relationships are built. Follow with a more "risky" revelation and gain confidence when they listen rather than blaming or shaming you. Gradually you'll see that some people are on your side and love you for who you are.

6. Release them

This may take a long time and can be done without your abusers ever knowing. Releasing your abuser is a transformational act you do for the sake of your own healing. It is not the same as condoning terrible behavior. It is an act of compassion toward yourself in which you also release yourself from the bond created when you hold on to resentment. When you release the toxic person, you let go of the ties that bind you to them. You don't have to make excuses for them, but if it helps, you can consider what happened in their own lives to make them behave this way.

As you rejoice in your own growth, feel sympathy for the way they stay stuck in their old patterns. You have evolved into a butterfly while they're stuck in their sticky cocoon. Your courage to establish an independent identity means you've given yourself unlimited possibilities for freedom and happiness. Your toxic family, on the other hand, stays mired in their mess, paralyzed by their fear of facing the simple truth that they need to make some changes. Once you see the truth of how small and powerless they are to you now, releasing them becomes easier.

CHAPTER FOUR

BOUNDARIES

> "'No' is a complete sentence."
>
> ANNE LAMOTT

THERE ONCE WAS A WOMAN who found it hard to say no. If someone asked her to do something, she felt obligated. As a result, she would do all kinds of things she didn't want to do; things other people might have enjoyed, but that made her unhappy. She had never learned to set boundaries, never heard of them. She didn't know it was her responsibility to teach people how to treat her. As a result, she felt misused as she put everybody's needs ahead of her own. The burden of pretending to be happy while doing mostly things that made her unhappy took a toll. She lost sight of what she liked and didn't like. It's hard to pursue your heart's desire when you have no idea what that is. So, she let other people design her life with their demands and she slowly disappeared.

If you haven't guessed already, that woman was me.

Maybe you can relate to having trouble setting boundaries. Even though your plate is full, you pile on more because someone asked you to. Or maybe they don't even have to ask. You take on more than is comfortable because you want to be seen as helpful or uncomplaining, or you know you need help but don't know how to ask for it. If you feel depleted and unsatisfied with life, that's a good sign you're sabotaging yourself through poor boundaries. If you turn to wine or other artificial soothers to help you feel better, that's another sign you're living in self-abandonment mode.

Having a lack of boundaries is often called "people-pleasing." Ironically, the behavior has less to do with a genuine desire to please others and more to do with a fear of their disappointment and disapproval. So, why do some people harbor such an irrational fear of the displeasure of others that they would desert themselves and their own needs? The answer lies, once again, in the past. If expressing basic wants and needs, or differences of opinion, got you punished or inspired your parents' rage, it makes sense you would be reticent to assert yourself as an adult.

If your parents failed to accept you or forgive you for your mistakes, you'll probably grow up to be a people pleaser. As a result of your parents' disapproval, you became hypervigilant about figuring out the needs of others and fulfilling them. If it feels unbearable to imagine someone being unhappy with you, that's a natural response to childhood trauma. When you were utterly dependent on your parents, their displeasure felt life-threatening to you. Even if they didn't beat you, the threat of their abandonment meant life or death to your developing brain. That same intensity of feeling carries through into adulthood and gets transferred onto people who are now your social equals.

Being Overly Apologetic

People-pleasing results in muddy communication and a lack of trust because others get the sense you're being dishonest about what you want and how you feel. One manifestation of this dishonesty is being overly apologetic. Have you ever found yourself apologizing for things that weren't your fault? Saying sorry too often can be a sign of poor boundaries. Apologizing unnecessarily chips away at your self-esteem and reinforces a negative self-image. It also influences the way others perceive you. There's evidence women apologize more than men as they're raised to be more polite and agreeable. A 2010 study by Schumann and Ross showed that men apologize less because they believe they commit fewer offenses worth apologizing for. According to this study, women have a lower threshold for what constitutes offensive behavior.

Living with the constant fear of offending people and how they might react creates a tremendous amount of anxiety and hypervigilance. It's natural to experience an elevated sense of anxiety when a threat arises. Then your system is supposed to calm down when the danger subsides. Hypervigilance happens when this heightened sense of arousal becomes your normal and your system has an impaired ability to soothe itself. The inner turmoil is an insidious form of self-abandonment that can result in chronic health issues.

If you grew up in a home that taught you to stay silent about your needs, you'll feel the need to say sorry anytime you ask for something. It may feel as though you're apologizing for your very existence. You were taught your opinions don't matter, so you find it hard to express them without saying sorry first. If you had authoritarian parents, you apologize as a sign of deference, even in adulthood.

If you weren't taught that you were important or that you mattered, you feel guilty for taking time for yourself and doing what you want, instead of what someone else wants. How do you feel when you have to say no to someone? Are you consumed with fears about what they'll think of you or that they'll get angry or reject you? Those fears instigate an apology to smooth the conflict you believe will ensue. It's a preemptive measure designed to prevent something that may never happen.

If you seek forgiveness for crying or expressing emotions, it's because you view your feelings as an inconvenience to others. But you're not imposing when you show up in the world as your authentic self. You're worthy of affirmation even when you're having a bad day. The quote often attributed to Marilyn Monroe says it well: "If you can't handle me at my worst, then you don't deserve me at my best."

On the plus side, you say sorry too often because compassion for others comes easily to you. But remember to reserve some of that compassion for yourself. Train yourself to stop anytime "sorry" threatens to fly out of your mouth. Then assess whether it applies in that situation.

Instead of saying sorry for arriving late, thank the person for their understanding, acknowledge that their time is valuable, and express gratitude for their patience. Rather than apologize for a late e-mail, thank the recipient for her patience while you took the time needed to write a considered response. You might find it useful to sit down with pen and paper and journal all the reasons you apologize. Seeing that faulty programming in black and white will give you incentive to stop apologizing so much.

Why It's Important to Set Boundaries

Setting boundaries is a matter of authenticity. It means being clear about what you want and don't want. It honors both yourself and the people around you. People aren't mind readers. That's why it's necessary to tell them how to treat you. You do that by being clear and setting boundaries in an unequivocal way. No explanation needed. As you practice saying no to things that don't serve you, it will become easier to do so without hedging. In the meantime, give yourself grace when you don't do it perfectly. Your confidence will increase as you find your choices align more with who you are. As a result, you'll be living a more authentic life.

Your opinion about yourself changes when you stop putting yourself last. When you overcome the subtle and not-so-subtle rejection that comes from living life on your own terms, you grow. You're like the proverbial eagle chick breaking her way out of the shell. All that lonely pecking helps the chick come out stronger. You begin to believe your needs matter and you have a responsibility to nurture those needs because they help you know how to serve the world.

How to Stop People-Pleasing

You must educate your brain to understand you won't die if people are displeased with you—and that most of them won't blame you for asserting your wants and needs honestly. In fact, they would expect nothing less. You also must accept the less pleasant fact that some of them won't take well to your new boundaries, and they aren't always on your side. Some are all too happy to take advantage of your unwillingness to stand up for yourself. That could be a sign they're struggling with their own issues, or they feel inconvenienced by the new you and are expressing those feelings honestly.

Either way, *that's not your problem.* Your job is to set healthy boundaries by honestly expressing your needs, not to predict how other people might react to them. It's certainly not to back down when they don't take it well. One of the hardest parts of setting boundaries is the disapproval you encounter from a small minority who don't want you to change. It's already excruciating work to set the boundary, then you come up against someone (probably with issues of their own) who wants to challenge it. This is where courage comes in. Some people will act disappointed because they can no longer depend on you to fulfill their unreasonable demands. They might get angry and try to persuade you to continue in your old patterns. These people are the reason you need boundaries. Their negative reaction is proof you're on the right path.

The first time I set a boundary with my father he got angry and gave hints he was going to distance himself from me. He had agreed to watch my children while I attended a recovery meeting a couple of weeks before Christmas. He had a habit of arriving two hours earlier than our scheduled time and that day was no exception. I braced myself as I answered the door, knowing I had to keep this promise to myself and set a boundary with him or nothing would change.

"I was expecting you in two hours," I said as he stood in the doorway. "I just sat down to watch a movie with the kids."

"Ah, well, I didn't have anything to do so I came early," he said as he pushed past me to make his way through the door.

"Well, I just sat down to watch a movie with the kids," I repeated. "I'd really prefer if you came back later."

"You want me to come back?" he said, incredulously.

"Yes, that would be better for me," I said.

He stood there for a moment, then shot me a disgusted look, shook his head, and to my surprise, he left. I did not expect him to return, but he did and looked after my children while I attended the meeting. But when I got home, he said he would leave the children's Christmas presents on the front step (whereas we would usually spend the holiday together). In spite of his response, I held my ground and by the time Christmas arrived, he came around. Most importantly, he never crossed that boundary again.

When you're a people-pleaser, it's incredibly difficult to feel like you're letting people down. Some of those people benefit from that guilt because it allows them to take advantage of you. If you never learned how to set boundaries, standing up for yourself feels wrong and selfish. It takes courage to overcome opposition and your own internal critic to design a life in line with your needs and values. (We'll talk about those in a minute.) If you're a people-pleaser, it feels easier to say yes to things. You'll suffer for a short time to keep the relationship or avoid disappointing someone. You'll do it simply to sidestep an uncomfortable conversation.

But this self-sabotaging mindset ensures you suffer and over-give in the long term. It never puts your relationships to the test. Boundaries in relationships help you discern whether someone takes an interest in your needs, or only wants you around for what you can do for them. You may never get comfortable saying no after a lifetime of saying yes, but you must do it anyway. Push through the discomfort because growth only happens outside your comfort zone. The amazing upside of saying no more often? Your yes becomes more meaningful and enjoyable. You feel great about helping others instead of obligated, burdened, and resentful.

If you're a person who requires solitude, let people know. Don't feel pressured to say yes to every social event just because it fits into your calendar. Pencil alone time into that calendar before you schedule anything else. On the flip side if you require variety and stimulation, take care of those needs, too. Spend time on hobbies that feed your passions, and projects that fulfill you. If doing less makes you feel bored, then incorporate more exciting ventures into your life. People don't know what you need until you tell them. And if you've lived a life for others, you may need time to discover your unique personality. You've buried your desires for so long, it may take time to uncover them again.

In this self-discovery phase, you'll spend more time journaling and writing down your likes and dislikes. You might decide to vacation alone if that's feasible for you or go on a retreat with like-minded people. Feed your longing for creativity with art projects. Take a class. Read books that inspire you. Spend more time in prayer or spiritual practice.

Understanding Your Values

To live a more intentional life, you must know what matters to you. If you are not clear on what you value, you'll be tossed to and fro rather than standing firm in your beliefs. Setting boundaries helps you align with your values (and perhaps discover them for the first time). When you get more deliberate about how you spend your precious resources of time and energy, you discover who you really are. When overcoming people-pleasing tendencies, it helps to define your values and use them as a filter through which you make decisions. I recommend drilling down to five core values, writing them down, and reviewing them regularly. You can find a simple test online to help you define yours. The one I use and recommend to clients is the Personal Values Assessment, which you can find at personalvalu.es. Ask questions about what makes you feel most like yourself, and what doesn't. In the process, you'll gain clarity over what matters most to you. Soon you'll begin to steer your life in that direction.

That nagging feeling of shame and guilt comes from a life lived in denial of your values. When you betray yourself with poor boundaries, it leaves you feeling bad about yourself. But you've been doing it so long you internalize this marker as a general sense of self-loathing.

Living outside your values is what leads to harmful self-soothing behaviors like drinking alcohol to excess and overeating. In extreme cases, it results in chronic illness and depression because you can only deny yourself so long before your body begins to protest.

Pruning

When you first start setting boundaries, you probably have so much in your life that's not working for you. You haul years of toxic baggage to the curb simply by saying no for the first time. Slowly removing things that don't serve you helps you figure out your likes and dislikes. You uncover who you are and what you value, and you begin to align your life with those things. If you're an introvert, you decline volunteering at a big event. If your goal is a house with less clutter, you stop to consider every purchase before you make it.

With practice, these boundaries become easier to set. You've removed all the garbage and reorganized what's left. You look around at a pristine castle and wonder how you can make it better. The castle is you, by the way. Instead of "Is this any good for me?," you begin to ask, "Is this the highest use of my talents and resources?" Bestselling author Henry Cloud uses pruning as an image to describe what I would call this level of boundary setting. Gardeners prune rosebushes to help them flourish. It involves cutting away healthy buds to give the best ones full access to the resources of the vine or bush.

Pruning enters your life once you get comfortable setting boundaries. You've cleared so much clutter from your head and your life. Now you no longer react to life but start creating one you love and make intentional choices to use your gifts for the greatest good. You examine your relationships and make the difficult decision to detach from people who prefer you kept quiet about your needs and served theirs instead. This is how healthy boundaries help you create a life aligned with your values and purpose.

CHAPTER FIVE

DEALING WITH TOXIC PEOPLE

"If you walked away from a toxic, negative, abusive, one-sided, dead-end, low vibrational relationship or friendship—you won."

LALAH DELIA

TOXIC PEOPLE haven't done the work of dealing with their internal issues and they harm the people in relationship with them. Nobody's perfect, but toxic people can really hold you back and make you question yourself. Their impact on your mental health can create anxiety, depression, sleeplessness, and loss of trust. The major areas where toxic people show up are in our families, romantic relationships, and in our workplaces; these are the areas we're going to cover in this chapter. First, here are four signs someone is toxic, though this is not an exhaustive list.

1. Toxic people can't tolerate vulnerability

Some toxic people pretend they have it all together. The act can be so convincing, even to themselves, you believe they don't have any problems. When you show vulnerability or try to share your struggles, they'll shut you down or change the subject because they can't handle this level of openness. That's because their image is more important than connecting with you or sharing a real relationship. People suffering with an avoidant attachment style would most closely resemble this type.

They might attack or pull away from you if you display a desire for connection. They make you the bad guy for wanting to share your struggles, which they portray as weakness or shameful. These people only tolerate positivity and tell you not to dwell on your problems. This is painful and confusing because it makes you believe there's something wrong with you for wanting to connect, or because you don't have it all together like they do.

2. Toxic people are selfish

It's all about them and their needs and when you bring up a problem, they immediately relate it to something in their own life. Suddenly, the conversation is all about them and you're wondering how this happened when you're the one who called asking for help. These types of toxic people are poor listeners uninterested in supporting you or discovering your needs. They can be the proverbial bottomless pit and no matter how much you give to them it's never enough. Selfish people can also be controlling because they don't know where they end and you begin. As far as they're concerned, everyone exists to serve their needs. Narcissistic people fall into this category.

3. Toxic people are critical

Toxic people don't give constructive criticism or helpful feedback. However they express it, they imply that you're not good enough and never will be. Many toxic parents fall into this category. They have an invisible standard you can't live up to. They let you know you're constantly disappointing them by falling short of that standard, but they never clue you into what you could do to meet their approval. These critical people look down on you, act superior to you, and chip away at your self-esteem with their constant complaints. But when you address the criticism or ask them how to be better, they deny that they've been critical at all.

4. Toxic people demand trust before it's earned

An example of this type is someone in a marriage who's had an affair and gets angry when you don't forgive them right away. They don't believe they should have to make changes in their behavior to help win your trust back. They think an apology should be enough. Another example is a spouse who betrays you financially by going into debt to make a bad investment without consulting you, and then balks at having his credit card activity monitored. He thinks you should trust him even though he's done nothing to earn it.

Trust needs to develop over time, even when someone has never betrayed you. More so when someone has broken your trust. People make mistakes and that's human, but if they're unwilling to pay the price to win back your trust, that's toxic. They might say, "If you loved me, you'd trust me." But you can still love someone and not trust them. That's healthy self-protection.

Toxic Family

Sometimes, the most toxic people in our lives are in our own families. My mother would call me at work to berate me, which would upset me and impact my productivity for the rest of the day. This is one small example of the myriad ways my mother's actions filled me with anxiety and self-doubt. Maybe you're stuck in such a situation right now and it's causing you a great deal of pain. The toxic family member treats you in emotionally damaging ways. Every interaction leaves you feeling ashamed and confused. They behave in bizarre ways, then hold you accountable for your normal reaction to that behavior.

There's no way to overestimate how difficult it can be to deal with toxic people in your family. Reasoning with toxic family members can feel impossible and, when you do, your worst fears about their reaction might come true. You may have been accepting their outrageous behavior because you've been primed to play this role with them for most or all of your life.

Starting with the least intense and ending with a last resort, here are three actions you can take to deal with your toxic family:

---

1. Voice your concern

Even when it seems futile, the first step is to tell them how you feel. Let them know you come away from interactions with them feeling bad and give recent examples of things they have said that hurt you. Ask them what they meant when they said those things. It's possible the person will respond positively to your query and will do the work to understand why they behave the way they do.

Unfortunately, this scenario is rare when toxic family members feel challenged. Bringing your concerns to the person, no matter how lightly you tread, may not have the desired effect. But it's a way of confirming to yourself that they are indeed toxic. If they acknowledge what you're saying about them and ask forgiveness, congratulations, but that's likely not going to be the case. That's because toxic people have no interest in changing. They point the finger at others and never at themselves. They will say you are too sensitive, imagining things, or lying about what they have said or done.

2. Limit contact

If they refuse to acknowledge your feelings and gaslight you, you'll benefit from limited contact and emotional detachment. An alternative to estrangement, this involves a psychic adjustment. It means relating to a family member in a new way. This solution is like the "gray rock" method of dealing with a narcissist. You respond non-emotionally rather than reacting. It is thought to demotivate the narcissist from viewing you as a target because you don't give him the "supply" he needs.

It means giving up the false hope that the person will change and protects you from getting pulled back into frustrating patterns and dysfunctional roles. The problem with this solution is the lack of authenticity, which can feel like a self-betrayal. So, even if it's not a good long-term measure for you, it buys you time to decide whether to continue the relationship for the long haul. Perhaps cutting off contact is not feasible, say in a divorce situation where you are forced to make co-parenting decisions about the kids.

3. Last resort: no contact

You've done your part by making the brave choice to confront the person about the emotional harm they've caused you. They've refused to acknowledge your feelings or the chance they could have done anything wrong. It's clear they care more about holding on to a false image of themselves than about their relationship with you. But limiting contact and detaching emotionally is not a viable long-term solution for you. Have you considered going no contact?

If you're ready for this step, then read on. No contact means no phoning, texting, or e-mailing them, and refusing to respond when they reach out to you. There's no need to tell anyone of your decision, but if you have trusted friends or family who would understand, enlist them to help you stay strong. You can tell the toxic person of your decision to end the relationship, but you don't have to. Based on their response to your truth telling, you may not want to expose yourself to more of their negativity and blame.

Going no contact will feel excruciating if you've become enmeshed or codependent. You'll need support from a counselor or understanding friend to help you follow through with your decision. Resist the urge to explain. You've done nothing wrong and don't need to defend yourself. Focus on moving forward rather than revisiting this dead-end relationship over and over.

Remind yourself how dangerous this person is to your personal growth and the life you envision for yourself. Stay strong!

Toxic Romance

Unlike our families, we get to choose our romantic partners. When you're getting to know someone, such as in a dating situation, it pays to take time to get to know the whole person. The more time you spend with toxic people, the more they reveal their negative character. The deeper you go in a relationship, the more you discover. That's why some suggest waiting at least a year after meeting before getting married.

To avoid self-sabotage in romantic relationships, keep an open mind and stay alert for red flags while in the courting phase. If you're a recovering people-pleaser, you're used to glossing over these signposts, or making excuses when they appear. But red flags don't go away because you ignore them. Rather, they get worse and more damaging to you. Think back to when you ignored such signs and ask yourself if that ever turned out well. These warning signals should be heeded at all costs.

Now that you've learned to set boundaries and have an idea of your values, you have some standards to guide you. Use those values as a filter through which you make decisions about new people in your life. Think about what you want rather than twisting yourself to fit into someone else's ideal. Dating is a weeding-out process whereby you eliminate candidates on your way to finding a suitable match. Reframe the narrative so that bad dates or poor matches are stepping stones that get you closer to finding the right one. See them as inevitable rather than a sign of failure.

Don't Overvalue Externals

We're attracted to people's external qualities at first. It's natural to be drawn to a person's looks, humor, charm, and achievements, but hold these initial attractions lightly and look deeper as you spend more time together. Internal qualities like integrity and honesty sustain a good relationship over time. A person of integrity is someone whose outside matches their inside. They're not one person at the beginning of the relationship and another once you get to know them. Again, think about your values and see if he or she shares many of them. Know your deal-breakers and stick to them.

Check Their Patterns . . . and Yours

Past behavior can be a good indicator of future behavior unless someone has done extensive personal growth work. Find out about this person's previous relationships by asking questions like how they ended and why. Listen to their answers to see if chaos seems to follow them around or they refuse to take responsibility. Is it always someone else's fault? Now look at yourself. Have you self-sabotaged by inviting toxic people into your life more than once in romantic relationships? If it happened once and you learned from the experience, that's healthy. However, if you get into relationships with these people repeatedly, something's wrong. You're ignoring or refusing to look at the warning signs. Maybe you're getting into relationships too quickly and failing to set appropriate boundaries to protect yourself.

Worst-Case Scenario:
The Romantic Con Artist

In extreme cases, failing to heed red flags can make you the victim of a con artist. Romantic con artists start with "love bombing," a common tactic among narcissists. That intense attention and affection that moves things too fast and prompts you to let down your guard is often manipulation. They pretend to like and dislike the same things you do to build a false sense in you of having found the perfect partner. Anyone can google your name or read your Facebook profile to find out all kinds of things about you. This is material they use to give you the false sense of feeling "known."

It's a popular and false belief that only the gullible fall for people who take advantage of them this way. In fact, those who fall for romantic scammers tend to be intelligent, educated, and successful. They are trustworthy and community oriented. In other words, they're good people who expect the same in others. These scammers seek out victims who are already lacking support and will isolate you further. If you have suffered a recent trauma, like divorce, you are more likely to fall for one. Firm boundaries like the ones below will help you avoid falling for nefarious types like these.

1. Don't commit too fast

Spend time with someone before becoming over-involved with them or giving your heart away. In the *Dirty John* true-crime podcast (later turned into a television series), John Meehan "love bombs" his victim, Debra Newell, who lets him move in after only five weeks and marries him a few short months later. After marriage, it became much easier for him to take advantage of her. He convinced her, a successful interior designer, to move them into a luxury $6,500 per month waterfront suite and, of course, foot the bill. He also neglected to tell her about his previous ten-year marriage that produced two children, and his time in prison for stealing drugs from the hospital where he worked.

2. Listen to what others say about him or her

And not only the positive comments. Listen to the friend or sister who points out his cracks or says she can't put her finger on why she doesn't trust him. Women's intuition is real and the woman who trusts hers is a gifted advisor. Pay attention to what she says. Debra's daughter warned her about John, saying she didn't like or trust him. She rightfully questioned why he always wore scrubs and had dirty fingernails when he claimed to be a medical professional. In reality, he never went to work because he had lost his license due to previous infractions.

3. Trust your own intuition

Most people who grew up in dysfunctional homes have spent their lives downplaying their intuition. This is because you've been taught to quiet that voice and do the bidding of your caregivers instead. Learn to listen to that voice inside you and heed those gut feelings. They mark the way to safety. I've learned that when my stomach says something's wrong, I need to pay attention. Ignoring your body's signals may have been necessary to survive childhood, but you're an adult now who needs to protect yourself. Avoidance will only make things worse and allow a dishonest person more opportunity to harm you.

4. If he seems too good to be true, he is

He claims to have a high-flying job but needs to borrow money. That's a huge warning sign and a common theme among romance scammers. He has the same interests as you and supports the same causes, but anyone could find those details on your Facebook profile or Instagram. He uses clichés that women love to hear but most men never say, like, "I can't take my eyes off you," or "You're the most amazing woman I've ever met." Be suspicious when someone says these things early on, like a first date. Pretending to fall for you immediately is the biggest romance scam of all.

Toxic People at Work

I used to work at a place where my department would meet for lunch every day and talk trash about everyone who wasn't there. I stayed silent until one day when I decided to take my lunches outside rather than stew in that toxic environment. When they confronted me about my absence, I said I needed to get out and walk around. During winter, I drove to the local mall and strolled around there. In summer, I went to a nearby park and enjoyed watching the ducks. Chances are you've had to deal with toxic people in the workplace at some point in your life. Maybe you're dealing with them now. In my career, I've experienced harassers, bullies, manipulators, and gossips. The stress of dealing with toxic coworkers can trigger self-sabotage by compromising your ability to do your job. Getting too close to toxic people in the office can also set you up for manipulation and backstabbing. The effects include but are not limited to:

- Decreased job satisfaction
- Lost sleep
- Low productivity
- Increased stress
- Poor mental health

How to Protect Yourself

Toxic coworkers keep you from fulfilling your goals because they hinder your productivity. They make work into another unsafe place in your life and increase stress levels, which impacts your health. We now know that family scapegoating and other childhood trauma can render you more susceptible to workplace bullying. So, how do you protect yourself?

Here are four ways to deal with toxic people in the workplace:

1. Find supporters

Form relationships with positive people in the office. You don't need to talk to them about the difficult person. Simply having good people on your side acts as an antidote to counter the effects of the toxic coworker.

2. Set boundaries

Do your best not to respond emotionally to the toxic coworker. Rise above their madness and refuse to get pulled down to their level. If it's the office gossip, socializer, or negative Nellie, tell them you can't talk right now, you're busy working. Use body language to indicate your unwillingness to engage with them. This could mean averting your eyes when they approach. Or you could wear headphones as a barrier.

3. Practice good self-care

Get a good night's sleep. You're more susceptible to someone's manipulation and other toxic tactics when you're not well rested. It's also essential for your overall well-being. Eating healthy and exercising regularly are two more ways to stay physically healthy and emotionally fit. They'll increase your confidence to counteract the negative effects of your coworker.

Meditation helps to keep your mind off the offending person and on the present moment instead. It also calms your brain and gives you more mental clarity. Meditation can take the form of prayer, breathing deeply, or sitting alone with your thoughts for a few minutes. The trick is to let the thoughts go by without judging them. Take time off for vacations and personal days when you can. It's important to get away to reset and refresh and take care of interests you have outside of work.

4. Focus on solutions

Rather than ruminate on things you can't control, focus on actions you can take. Instead of dwelling on the problem of the toxic person, think of ways you can manage them and maintain your sanity. There's no point trying to understand the mind and motives of a toxic coworker as they are often driven to get their way at any cost. Don't bother reasoning with them because they only know how to deflect blame. If you do complain, they might manipulate the situation to make you look bad. So, arm yourself with evidence by documenting dates and times of offenses. Stick to the facts if you are forced to bring in human resources.

Sometimes, the best way to protect yourself means staying silent. Unlike a toxic friend or family member, you can't go no contact with someone at work. But you can adjust your mindset to prevent the situation from affecting your productivity and mental health. In extreme cases, you may choose to look for another job. It's not fair, but sometimes avoiding self-sabotage means making big changes in the name of self-preservation.

CHAPTER SIX

OVERCOMING NEGATIVE SELF-TALK

"Don't believe everything
you tell yourself."

LIDIA LONGORIO

DID YOU KNOW your inner voice reflects how your parents and other authority figures talked to you when you were a child? In addition, the harsh self-critic arises as a defense mechanism against (perceived) inevitable punishment. It protects us from hurt by lowering our expectations. Some people suggest counteracting the negative voice with a positive one. However, I believe action works better in helping us develop a healthy self-narrative. Besides, research has shown that positive mantras can make us feel worse if unaccompanied by a genuine sense of self-worth.

Treating yourself like you matter and adopting good self-discipline habits will create an authentic change in your internal voice rather than mere behavior modification. Many people report feeling surprised by a newly encouraging voice that arises in their head because of their personal development work. Before I began my healing journey, I could not remember one time in my life when my inner voice spoke nicely to me. The first time that voice said something encouraging, it stopped me in my tracks. *Who was that?* I thought. The change came as a natural response to the new ways I'd begun to treat myself. Now when I catch myself thinking, *You're so stupid* (which still happens from time to time), I counter that voice with a corrective, *No, you made a mistake.* Because now, I believe it's true. If I had started with positive self-talk with nothing to back it up, I don't think it would have created the same lasting change.

How to Stop Negative Self-Talk

Start with Self-Compassion

Self-compassion is simply offering yourself the same level of support and understanding you would a friend or family member. You may have noticed that the criticism you heap on yourself is unmatched. You'd never berate someone else for making a mistake the way you do yourself, or call them a failure for falling short of a goal. If you pay attention to your internal voice, you may be shocked at how harshly and cruelly you speak to yourself. If you tend to criticize rather than comfort yourself when you're going through something hard, you need more self-compassion in your life. Kristin Neff, PhD, the foremost researcher on the topic and author of *Self-Compassion*, defines self-compassion as kindness and understanding toward yourself in the face of your perceived personal failings. Here are the three key ways she says we can demonstrate self-compassion.

1. Kindness toward yourself

It's common to jump to self-criticism when you feel you're falling short. You push harder rather than extending yourself grace. You forget to go easy on yourself when you are weary and need rest. Rather than comforting yourself the way you would a friend when you're going through something difficult, you berate yourself. How many times have you told yourself you "shouldn't feel that way"? Self-compassion says to acknowledge and accept your feelings without judgment. Be kind to yourself when things don't turn out the way you expected or when you fail at something that was important to you. Failure means you tried and it's a necessary step on the road to success.

You may worry that being too nice to yourself will prevent you from reaching your goals. If that were true, you wouldn't need to read this book. If being mean to yourself helped you reach your goals, you should have everything you want right now. In fact, this limiting belief may live in your subconscious mind as another secret saboteur that prevents you from enjoying your life. You may be re-creating patterns from childhood in which you had to rely on yourself to get your needs met. You feared dropping the ball because you had too much responsibility and that led to fierce hypervigilance. You may also be echoing the voices of your parents and other authority figures who gave you criticism instead of kind words. You have no model for treating yourself nicely, but we're going to change that.

2. Shared human experience

When something bad happens, are you convinced you're the only person in the world who feels this way? The tendency to isolate when you're going through something hard exacerbates your pain and contributes to the ruminating thoughts that keep you stuck. This happens when you replay over and over events that cause you distress, without acting to find a solution. You might fall into the trap of feeling inadequate for making a mistake, but everyone falls short sometimes. When you're going through a difficult time, it's important to remember that everybody goes through those times. When you fail at something, you're in good company because we all fail at times. It's in our sufferings and shortcomings that we find connection with others. Rather than letting your downtimes separate you from the world, use them to create bonds of intimacy.

Have you noticed that when you share something difficult it inspires the other person to reveal something vulnerable about themselves? You might be surprised at the response you get when you take the risk to be vulnerable. Reaching out to others is a form of self-compassion and relationships deepen when you risk sharing something hard or embarrassing. You may have been raised to believe you're on your own with your difficult emotions. You may have also gotten the message that you have to be perfect to earn love and acceptance.

Your inner child's desire to isolate you comes from the need to protect you from the pain of that rejection. However, as an adult you can re-parent that inner child by taking the risk to share your emotional world with someone else. Even if you do get rejected, you will survive and grow from the experience. You'll get information about the people in your life that comes from these tests of intimacy. If they cannot deal with your emotional honesty, they may not be someone you can lean on in times of need. This is difficult to acknowledge but helpful to know as you seek to surround yourself with people who elevate and support you.

3. Feeling all your emotions

We tend to identify certain emotions as positive and others as negative. We celebrate joy and victory and push down other states of mind that don't feel as good. But all our emotions have something to tell us. It's necessary to engage with them fully to enjoy a healthy, balanced life. When you feel all your feelings, you neither minimize nor blow them out of proportion and you stop overidentifying with them. Think *I feel sad* instead of *I am sad*.

You accept these feelings and let them give you the messages they're designed to give. Then, you can take that information and apply it to your future. For example, anger serves as a wonderful catalyst for change. It tells you what's not working and inspires you to set boundaries and advocate for yourself. If you feel regret, rather than berating yourself, decide to do things differently next time. Approach your feelings with a spirit of curiosity and nonjudgment and remember, they are all valid.

Accept the gentle lessons and stop beating yourself up for being human. That's how your life becomes more aligned with who you are. Your self-image increases and as a result your inner narrative becomes more positive. Forgive yourself for past mistakes and acknowledge you did the best you could with the information you had. Extend compassion to yourself for the ways your past influenced your future actions. Determine to learn from those experiences, then release them. Accepting your feelings helps you take the lesson that often gets lost when you're consumed with self-inflicted guilt and shame.

Embrace Internal Motivation

Internal motivation means doing something because it pleases or fulfills you in some way. You tune out what people might think and tune into what you desire. In contrast, external motivators prompt us to seek rewards outside ourselves, like recognition and approval from others. While external validation is not always wrong, we need to keep it in check. When your main drivers are external, your values misalign with who you are inside, and your moral compass becomes skewed. This results in poor boundaries and making decisions that sabotage you in an effort to please or impress others.

An overly external focus reduces your self-image and contributes to your negative self-talk. It leaves you feeling powerless and with little control over your life. Have you noticed how fretful you feel when you focus on the behavior of other people, such as family members who mistreat you? When you turn the focus on yourself, however, you can begin to meet your needs in a way that lowers your anxiety and increases your ability to deal with those difficult others.

Paying attention to your present-moment needs dials down the overwhelming sense of frustration that comes when you think of all the things you can't control. Internal focus also dispels the need for support and understanding from people who are not on your side. When you turn the lens away from people society says are *supposed* to love and care for you and turn it instead on yourself and meeting your own needs, you find freedom. Here are three ways to know when your external motivation is out of balance and what to do about it.

1. Lack of joy

In our culture, if you love something and are good at it, people assume you should seek to be paid for it. For example, I first started blogging for the sheer pleasure of writing, researching, and learning how to develop a new platform. After a couple of years of consistent posting, companies started dropping into my e-mail with requests for me to write sponsored posts. It seemed like a dream to blog for money, but it meant I had to gear the content toward the advertiser's needs.

Writing my blog for money took away the pleasure and made it into a chore. It no longer fulfilled me or gave me a creative outlet because I had to cater to other peoples' needs instead of my own. This external motivation compromised my integrity and removed the joy for me, so I released the sponsors and went back to blogging for myself and my reader. When you do something for the fulfilment and love of it, that isn't necessarily a sign you have to make a living from it. Internal motivation says creative fulfillment can be payment enough.

2. You're focused on recognition

Are you setting goals based on what others will think of you? Instead of checking in with your heart's desire, you think about how much others will admire you. The status and recognition of achieving the goal attract you more than the personal fulfillment.

If it weren't for the accolades, there's no way you'd pursue this goal. However, when you're overly focused on this type of external validation, the process of achieving a goal will soon lose its luster.

If you're more interested in the external reward that only comes once you've achieved something, you're more likely to give up before you arrive there. It will be hard to maintain the stamina needed to push through all the tedious tasks that precede success. If you're more interested in fame than the creative process, for example, performing in obscurity will seem intolerable. You'll give up before reaching your goals, further feeding into the negative self-image and self-talk. When you derive pleasure from the work itself, however, you'll enjoy the process whether or not you become well-known as a result.

3. You refuse to take risks

If you refuse to take risks due to fear of failure or how others will perceive you, that's external motivation, too. You might be worried what people will think if you say your goal out loud, which only reduces your chances of getting there. When you avoid trying something new because of how others might react, you lose the opportunity to know yourself better. You've attached your self-worth to what others think or even what you think they think (that is, projection). Therefore, your work, and by extension, you, are worthy only if other people like and approve.

This holds you back from expressing yourself fully and deprives the world of your uniqueness. Rather than bringing your creativity and new ideas, you show what you think is safe and will likely receive praise (which means we've probably seen it before). The answer: take the risk to do what you were created to do. The short-term discomfort will pay off in long-term life satisfaction and fulfillment.

Letting Go of Perfectionism

Perfectionism is more than a cute character trait that makes you a little hard on yourself. In fact, it shares many of the characteristics of unresolved childhood trauma, like setting unreasonably high expectations for oneself, a loud inner critic, fear of making mistakes, and trouble trusting others. Perfectionists can't tolerate mistakes; they engage in black-and-white thinking, and struggle to meet challenges required to achieve big goals. So, perfectionism is more serious than many of us think. It could well be a conditioned response to a childhood in which you never felt good enough.

As we've learned, children who've been traumatized grow up with brains that can't tolerate making mistakes. They've been rewired to be more rigid and controlling, less trusting of others, and less equipped to face challenges and accomplish goals. As an antidote, allow yourself to do things badly at first. My greatest lesson as a writer came in learning to write initial drafts. Also known as "vomit drafts," these firsts have one purpose: to get words out of you and onto the page. You can edit these later, but you can't improve on something that doesn't exist.

The need to be perfect paralyzes you; you fear making mistakes and coming up short, so you fail to begin at all. This leads to underachievement and disappointment with yourself. Cue more negative self-talk. Your inner critic never seems to let you off the hook as you compare yourself to others and come up short. Never mind that others have decades of experience you don't. You feel as though you must get it right the first time. Perfectionists expect too much from themselves. More than that, they underestimate how long and how difficult it will be to achieve a goal.

The perfectionist believes success should come at the first attempt. If you were never taught the importance of perseverance, you may not realize how many years and decades of effort are required to attain the excellence you seek. Media likes to celebrate the overnight success but glosses over the less glamorous climb to the top. Even among us regular folk, many present an image of success that may not match what goes on behind the scenes. The "fake it till you make it" mentality our society encourages can prevent us from sharing the struggles that inevitably come before sustained success.

As a result, you view failure as fatal instead of a necessary rung on the ladder of life. If you were punished or rejected for mistakes or failures, you will fear these and avoid them as an adult. You may believe failing or falling short at one thing means you are a failure or incapable of success. If you study successful entrepreneurs, however, you will see their many failures only drove them further in their quest to succeed. Instead of letting failure say something about them, they took the lessons and applied them to future endeavors to perform more effectively. Sometimes, their businesses did fail, but they started another one rather than throw their hands up.

Celebrate your attempts and failures and see them as growth opportunities and necessary steps on the road to success. Stop looking ahead for one hot minute and look back at what you've done well in your life (or good enough). Congratulate yourself not for your achievements, but because you took a chance. Besides providing lessons, failure provides evidence of courage. Begin to value that courage more than accomplishment, approval, or recognition. Find people who are supportive and remind you of all the good qualities you possess, and spend less time with those (including your family) who speak to you unkindly or criticize you. Surround yourself with like-minded people who understand that a fulfilling life of integrity requires a certain amount of risk. Letting go of what people think and following instead what fulfills you will go miles toward reducing the inner critic. You move away from the world's definition of success and closer to your own.

CHAPTER SEVEN

ADOPTING HEALTHY COPING MECHANISMS

"The attempt to escape from pain,
is what creates more pain."

DR. GABOR MATÉ

I HAD USED ALCOHOL since high school to ease my self-loathing and constant unease. Even before I became a daily drinker, I'd anticipate weekends when I could binge drink and find a break from the bad feelings. Alcohol became the support I never had, allowing me to put down my shoulders after a long day of wrestling with the world. Without the skills to navigate life's challenges, alcohol provided a respite from the constant hypervigilance that mentally and physically exhausted me.

Rather than intervening, my family and friends seemed more interested in helping me cover up and make excuses for my habitual imbibing. When I asked a friend if she thought I had a drinking problem, she replied, "The fact you're asking that means you don't." I can only guess enabling me allowed them to avoid looking at their own drinking patterns and maintain the status quo. I now know that enabling is a primary way dysfunctional family members keep the broken system going. Rather than helping an individual, they gloss over the problem in a "nothing to see here" fashion; or scapegoat the individual and apply shame, blame, and guilt rather than understanding and empathy. In this way, families can keep their image intact while pointing the finger at one "broken" person and absolving themselves of responsibility.

Like most coping mechanisms, what may have been adaptive at first became wholly maladaptive as life wore on. As children, we survive impossible circumstances by finding ways to soothe ourselves from the constant pain we experience. Since no one taught us how to care for ourselves in healthy ways (or that our needs mattered), we do what it takes to feel better. However, feeling better in the moment is often a recipe for disaster in the long run. Unlike many other drugs, alcohol kills slowly. This allowed me to function within my addiction for decades without intervention, and the consequences began to pile up.

I became beholden to alcohol in a way that made it feel impossible to live without it. I stopped asking friends if they thought I had a problem and began hiding my drinking lest someone try to take it away from me. I now refused to admit I had a problem because that would mean I would have to give it up, and to me that had become inconceivable. I didn't always drink to excess, but I relied on alcohol to be there for me whenever I needed a break from reality. Like an unfaithful lover, it gave me a temporary respite from pain while adding new agony to the mix. Apologizing for emotional outbursts and lying about injuries sustained while under the influence became my norm. Hangovers ruled my day and I never felt as though I was operating at full capacity. It got to the point where I was either drunk or recovering from a hangover almost every moment of the day.

Some say those who fall prey to addictions lack willpower. But at the height of my alcohol dependence, I trained for and completed a marathon. I monitored my caloric intake and never gained an ounce of fat. Appearing perfect seemed important on a life-and-death level because I felt I had nothing else to offer. It's no coincidence that the only rare praise I received from my parents pertained to my looks. A perfect appearance became my minimum standard for taking up space in society. I would not allow myself to go out without hair and makeup done and a carefully chosen outfit. I wondered how others could walk around looking the way they did, not in a critical manner but with a sense of wonder. I knew the confidence required to look less than perfect in front of others did not belong to me.

Running helped me keep the weight off, and it also prevented me from drinking myself into oblivion. I knew if I had to wake up and run fifteen miles, I would drink less and leave the party early. These are the lengths I had to go to to curb my alcohol use, proving I had no lack of self-discipline. Similarly, when I become pregnant with each of my two children, I ceased drinking and took it back up the moment they arrived into the world. I lost all the baby weight within three months by sticking to a strict diet and exercise regimen. By the same token, other substance abusers have shown immense productivity at work. They have the seeming self-control to excel in their professional lives, even while lacking the same control with their Achilles' heel.

As a result of these inconsistencies, I no longer believe in the concept of a powerful will. The trait is simply too selective to be real. For example, someone who binge eats can easily resist an alcoholic beverage and vice versa. Unfortunately, much of the self-help advice around improving your habits stresses the importance of willpower. As you may well know, the desire to stop is rarely enough to keep us away from our compulsive behaviors. Here are five reasons why:

1. Willpower runs out

Willpower doesn't work because it's a finite resource. That's why trying to stop drinking using so-called self-discipline is a fool's errand. It's called *white knuckling* in the recovery space and ends in a relapse. This misguided belief in willpower is the same reason dieters most often gain back all the weight they lost and more. With nothing guiding you but a strong will, as soon as you let your foot off the brake pedal, you go speeding headlong toward the end of your good intentions.

2. Willpower is not fun

Using willpower to overcome an indulgence signals to our brains deprivation and lack. We feel we're missing out on something, and we are. We're denying ourselves the pleasure of a decadent dessert after a hearty meal. We watch our friends enjoy the conviviality brought on by strong drink while we stay stone-cold sober. Unless we experience the benefits of kicking our habit, our brains will not allow us to stop. Unfortunately, lost pounds or sobriety are not compelling enough reasons, especially for those of us whose brains have not been wired to view the long game.

Remember that survival brain we talked about that keeps us focused on present threats? That brain is not concerned with the long-term benefits of your new habit; it needs to keep you safe now and will do so at all costs, even when it means harming you in the long run. The true benefit that will make us change is much deeper than a slim figure or the fulfilment of a promise to a weary spouse. It's truth and authenticity and the resolution of past trauma, but we're not taught to look for those.

3. Willpower ignores the real problem

The cult of willpower says you are the problem and if you weren't so lazy, undisciplined, and consumed with immediate gratification, you'd enjoy a life free from your compulsive behaviors. It's a neat trick that lets so many off the hook and puts you there instead. It removes accountability from your parents and caregivers who failed to meet your needs or give you the tools you needed to cope. It removes culpability from a society that encourages us to ignore our feelings and get on with the business of productivity and consumption. The real reasons we escape into our coping mechanisms get ignored when we talk about willpower.

4. Shame is the driving force of willpower

Thanks to people like Brené Brown, it's become more well-known that shame is ineffective for driving change. All it does is make people go underground, hiding their bad habits and transgressions. When we shame people into thinking they could stop if they had better character, they start keeping secrets to avoid judgment.

The coping mechanism now offers relief from that shame, and will-power can't overcome the need to escape those damning feelings.

5. Willpower is isolating

Willpower means depending on yourself and no one else. That's why twelve-step recovery programs thrive instead on group therapy and leaning on a higher power. Most addicts who eventually recover have tried to get sober or clean on their own and failed. By the time I entered recovery rooms I had dozens of relapses behind me. My willpower had even helped me to stop drinking for five whole months under my own steam. But it wasn't until I entered recovery that I stopped drinking for good, or at least a dozen years ago and counting. That's because the program gave me permission to say I was powerless against alcohol. It invited me to speak honestly about my addiction with others who had been there. And it never shamed anyone regardless of what they had done or how many relapses they encountered while in recovery.

Many of us grew up receiving little empathy and compassion from our parents or caregivers. Because no one helped us feel better when we were hurting, we find it hard to soothe ourselves or even to know what we need to help us feel better today. You may feel confused about self-care and have trouble determining what you need. That's because you've been primed to shut off your desires and intuition rather than tune into them. I've had clients who say practicing self-care makes them feel lazy, lonely, and even worthless. That's because caring for yourself when you've been conditioned to ignore your needs feels dangerous. It means letting down the guard that has kept you safe. It means feeling unproductive when producing may have been the only way you received love.

You thought about ways to make things easier for your parents and to be less of a burden. Your parents were allowed to have temper tantrums or make mistakes, but you weren't. They never had to apologize or make amends, but you always did. Maybe, as an older sibling, you were forced to become a caregiver for the younger ones. Putting an older sibling in the role of caregiver has been normalized in our society, but that doesn't make it right.

It leads to over-responsibility in adulthood and overdependence by younger siblings who assume you're there to cater to their needs. This pattern of sibling inequality can carry on throughout a lifetime.

Wherever you are in the birth order, when you grow up learning to put other people first, to not ask for help, and to minimize your own needs, you will have an underdeveloped sense of self-compassion. Your family may have undervalued your thoughts and feelings and refused to see you as an individual or treat you as a whole person at all. Even when all your material needs were taken care of, emotional neglect had the same damaging effect on your developing psyche as physical abuse.

Your survival depended on you tuning into what others wanted rather than your own needs. When you grow up with unmet needs, you become acutely attuned to the needs of others while abandoning your own needs and wants. If expressing needs, either emotional or physical, got you punished or rejected by your caregivers, that felt life-threatening to your little nervous system. When you were dependent on the adults around you for your very survival, rejection from them could feel like death. So, you did whatever you could to keep them happy.

As we enter adulthood, our peers take the place of our parents as the objects of our hypervigilance. Rather than seeking to share intimacy with new friends, you desperately try to figure out what they want so you can give it to them, and then they won't leave you. Same goes for new romantic attachments where you ignore red flags others would spot in a moment. You're so busy trying to get them to like you, you miss the things about them that will potentially hurt you. It's like going into battle without armor or a shield. You are inviting someone to maim or even kill you—and I mean that in a literal sense. Romantic con artists like the one in *Dirty John* prey upon people with few or no boundaries. The woman at the center of that drama kept overlooking and making excuses for John's obvious lies as he infiltrated her family and eventually attempted to murder her daughter.

Instead of paying attention to your own feelings, you monitored theirs. Instead of asking for help, you made yourself as small as possible to avoid becoming a burden. As a result, you became disconnected from your emotional and physical needs. Your survival depended on you becoming an expert at knowing what other people need and giving them that. That's why you may have empathic qualities and take on other peoples' emotions in a way that feels overwhelming at times. Healthy self-soothing feels insufficient to fill the gaping hole left by your unmet childhood needs, so you're forced to find comfort by more extreme means. Something as simple as knowing what you need from moment to moment becomes a skill you must learn in order to take care of yourself.

This constant tuning out from your own needs and tuning into others has led to the unhealthy coping mechanisms you use to try to escape bad feelings. These include substance and behavioral addictions like drugs and alcohol, shopping, gambling, pornography, and too many comfort foods. Instead of the mild distraction and stress relief that healthy self-care provides, you go for things that obliterate your feelings and numb you out so you can experience a complete break with reality. Instead of a release valve that lets off a little steam, you wait until you're completely pressurized and can no longer cope without a drastic alteration of your state of mind and being. This is the nature of an addiction.

The conditioning you received to disconnect from your feelings and intuition make it difficult for you to self-soothe any other way because you have no idea what you want or need. In addition, you are out of touch with when your body and mind need relief—it is only at the breaking point that you finally acquiesce. At that point, run-of-the-mill self-care strategies are simply not enough to give you the relief you need. *Get me out of here!* your body is crying, and a bubble bath is not potent enough to do that. This makes sense when you've been conditioned to ignore your desires and cater to others' instead.

To avoid your parents' rage or disapproval, you suppressed or ignored these needs and did your best not to have any. Rather than ask for help and risk rejection, you tried to take care of these needs yourself. In childhood, this was an intelligent skill that helped you survive. If speaking up would have been dangerous for you, staying quiet is a smart way to keep yourself safe. However, as an adult you continue minimizing your needs and prioritizing the needs of others in a way that has become maladaptive. This leads you to treat others better than you do yourself—even today. So how do you begin to change this habit of disconnecting from yourself and tuning into others? How do you reverse this dynamic so you can take care of yourself effectively and appropriately?

The first step is to face the truth. Have you been using an unhealthy substance or behavior to soothe yourself in the short term, and have you come to rely upon that? If so, there's no shame in admitting that. In fact, shame will only compound the problem. As someone who depended on alcohol and binge eating to get by, I can attest that shame only made my problems worse. Remember how I stopped sharing my concerns over my drinking and started to hide it? As soon as a habit goes underground, there's trouble. When you isolate yourself with your habit, it will likely become too big for you to handle. That's why the first step in my recovery program was to admit that my dependence on alcohol had become "unmanageable."

If you grew up in a home where your needs went unmet, how to self-soothe will not come naturally. Your parents did not comfort you when you experienced pain, either emotional or physical. More often, they were the source of that pain and to assuage their own guilt, shame, or fear of intimacy you had to make them feel better by minimizing your self-expression. Unlike healthy parents and caregivers, yours were not interested in helping you develop into the unique individual you were born to be. More likely, they viewed you as an extension of themselves or as a burden and an inconvenience. They proved that every time they looked at you with contempt. Of course, this is a result of their own childhood trauma, but we are focused here on how that affected you and not extending ever more sympathy to your parents.

I'm willing to bet you've had no end of people, including therapists, who remind you not to blame your parents and that forgiveness is the only path to healing. They say your parents "did the best they could with what they had." While I question the blanket truth of that statement, I accept that it may be accurate in some cases. However, that is beside the point. We have been too focused on our parents and caregivers all our lives. That is a large part of why we find ourselves where we are, in lives where our own needs get abandoned in favor of what others need and want from us. I propose we take the focus off our parents and place it on ourselves, not in a narcissistic fashion but in a way that helps us meet our own needs today.

How do you apply self-care when you're uncertain what it is you actually need? You've been so conditioned to detach from your needs that attending to them feels scary and even impossible. Denying your needs is how you survived childhood and it worked quite well because . . . you're here. But those coping mechanisms that were highly intelligent and adaptive in childhood become maladaptive in adulthood. They hold us back in all areas of our lives—career, relationships, health, and finances.

For example, flying under the radar that kept you safe from dad's rages plays out as a fear of speaking up at meetings, which means you fail to get acknowledged for your ideas. It results in an unwillingness to ask for a deserved promotion or raise, which directly impacts your level of income. As for health, the constant suppression of anger can cause disease in the body, according to Dr. Gabor Maté who wrote about the concept in the book *When the Body Says No.* If you refuse to speak up for what you want, or share your thoughts, feelings, and opinions, your relationships will fail to flourish. The intimacy you no doubt crave and have missed all your life will continue to elude you.

When it comes to taking care of yourself, you're at a loss as to what to do because it is simply not something that was ever given to or modeled for you. It's like asking someone who's never watched a baseball game to get out there and hit a home run. They don't even know the rules of the game. They've never held a bat or thrown a ball. What is a catcher's mitt, exactly? Before you can play the game well, you have to practice the fundamentals; same goes for self-care.

Without the benefit of having learned the basics of self-care, you go for quick, unhealthy fixes to feel better. As you know, these unhealthy practices do little to help you feel better in the long run. They may offer a quick dopamine hit but leave you feeling guilty and empty inside. In fact, they compound the bad feelings you're already grappling with by tossing shame into the mix. They then add a healthy dose of negative consequences that sabotage your success in all areas of your life.

These short-term quick fixes do nothing to fill you up the way healthy self-care would and that's part of the reason why they're not sustainable. Rather than engaging in consistent self-care so that your tank is full, you wait until you're running on empty. Only then do you desperately look for solutions to the problems of anxiety, exhaustion, or [insert your brand here of] discomfort. That's not your fault; it's an extension of the survival mechanisms you used in childhood. As mentioned, these worked very well for you at one time, but that time has passed.

Developing Self-Compassion

A big part of overcoming shame includes developing the self-compassion we discussed in the previous chapter. This means caring about yourself the way you care about others. You offer yourself the same level of support and kindness you would a friend or family member. Practice asking yourself what you want or what's best for you the next time someone asks you for something. You are likely so used to looking outward and pleasing others that this simple turning within to tune into your own needs feels unnatural. It may not occur to you to ask what you need in these situations, but it's essential if you want an authentic life where you get your needs met.

The second pillar of self-compassion, common humanity, reminds you that you're not alone in your struggles. The isolation that comes from shame about your unhealthy coping mechanisms only exacerbates them. You may be used to going through things on your own, but you may have noticed that has not helped you heal. When you try to cope on your own with unmanageable feelings, your world gets smaller. This is why the world seems so scary to someone with a disorganized attachment style (see Chapter 2). You stay stuck in survival mode where much of your life is spent hiding and covering up your habits rather than reaching out for help. When you've reached out in the past you didn't receive the help you needed because you asked the wrong people. These could have been the destructive people in your life whom you've chosen based on the false self you're presenting to the world. Or it could have been therapists untrained in trauma recovery or complex PTSD who didn't have the skills to help you.

Now that you know where your unhealthy patterns stem from, you can ask questions to qualify therapists before you start working with one. Have they heard of complex PTSD? The term, coined by Judith Herman, author of *Trauma and Recovery*, refers to the syndrome that follows prolonged and repeated traumas rather than a single traumatic event. Have they worked with anyone who's struggled with it? You may have stayed with an ineffective course of therapy because you believed it was your fault the therapy wasn't working. Considering your past, this makes tremendous sense if you transferred the role of parent onto the counselor.

As with your parent, you decided you needed to please them to earn a space in their office (even though you paid for the privilege). You may have felt tempted to give the right answers to help the therapist feel like she was doing a good job. It may not have occurred to you that you had the right to switch counselors or that it's possible they were a poor fit. You are so used to blaming yourself and putting up with situations that don't serve you, you extended that pattern to your experience on the therapist's couch.

It's important to remember that a mental health professional works for you and not the other way around. Besides qualifications there needs to be a good interpersonal fit. Remember that therapists are people, too, and they can be narcissistic, disrespectful, or lack compassion like any other person. The title does not automatically make someone a trustworthy person. Like anyone else, a therapist needs to earn your trust and the good ones will want to do that. Dr. Sherrie Campbell, a clinical psychologist in California, says trust is not something given but earned, and you should always start at ground zero with anyone you don't know.

If you transfer the parental role onto your new therapist and then neglect to protect yourself by requiring them to earn your trust, you risk being re-traumatized. Rather than relief from the pain of your childhood, you will experience a deep cut into the same wound that can feel devastating. For this reason, talk therapy is not always the answer for complex PTSD survivors and can make the problem worse. The research of Dr. Peter Levine showed that soldiers with PTSD who talked about their experiences over and over with a therapist experienced a worsening of their symptoms. He found that a more body-oriented, somatic approach worked better. Similarly, you may have better success with other forms of therapy and find that working with a trauma-informed coach suits your needs more closely. Don't let a bad experience with therapy make you believe the help you need is not out there, or there is something wrong with you, or that you are unfixable.

The third pillar of self-compassion, mindfulness versus over-identification, means when hard feelings come, you acknowledge them without either suppressing or exaggerating them. Observe your feelings without judgment and look at them realistically. You may be used to talking yourself out of so-called negative feelings by telling yourself you "shouldn't" feel that way or by giving yourself a pep talk. Neither of these approaches shows self-compassion because they deny you the right to your honest emotions. If you can accept your feelings and sink into them without making it mean anything about you, you'll understand that feelings happen to you, but they do not define you. Self-compassion means giving yourself the grace to acknowledge your feelings rather than escaping them through unhealthy coping mechanisms.

When we haven't learned self-compassion, we turn to unhealthy substitutes. How many moms do you know who use wine for comfort because they're missing what they really need, which is sleep and time alone or something deeper? There's a whole meme culture devoted to this very topic. It's not self-compassionate to avoid your feelings by drinking, binge-watching, or numbing out in some other way. Though it may feel better in the short term, it does nothing to improve your life or to relieve you from the pain of your situation. So, how do you incorporate healthy self-soothing into your life, and how can you stop sabotaging yourself with unhealthy coping mechanisms?

1. Get honest with yourself

It's possible you've come to depend on one or more of these coping strategies at the level of an addiction. We can become addicted to behaviors like shopping and gambling as much as substances such as alcohol or food. Our culture has a relaxed attitude toward drinking, but if you're dependent on alcohol that's no laughing matter. The emotional and physical health risks of drinking too much are underplayed in our society, possibly because it is such a cash cow. Altering your state of mind rather than facing your issues, however, will ensure things never change.

Instead of looking for the escape hatch, begin to process the reality of your emotions by simply paying attention to them. This is how you get to know yourself better and learn how to attend to your true needs. Then you can begin to let go of the unhealthy coping mechanisms that served you in childhood and learn to meet your own needs now through healthy self-soothing. You may have to get help and do some internal work to get out from under dependence on any of previously mentioned behaviors, but it's the only way to move forward.

2. Look at your triggers

What precedes your turning to your favorite unhealthy coping mechanisms? Is there a thought, feeling, or action that happens directly prior to you seeking relief in the form of a drink, binge, or other outlet? Simply paying attention to the trigger helps you feed the real need while staying present. You have to learn to give yourself the feeling of being seen and known when it is something your parents have denied you. Rather than going along with your pattern of escaping reality, get curious about what happens directly before to create a more conscious approach to self-care. When you feel the urge to escape through an unhealthy coping behavior, stop and ask yourself what you really need. Lean into the feelings instead of running away from them.

3. Go further than skin deep

You may have thought of self-care as a mani-pedi, or a warm bath with candles—and that's why it never worked for you. Those superficial practices were not nearly potent enough to cover over the deep wounds you dealt with as a survivor of childhood trauma. Now you know self-care goes deeper than that: it means taking care of your need for connection to yourself, God, and others. Perhaps you need time alone to free-write what's on your mind. You'll be amazed at what comes to the surface with only ten minutes of unstructured journaling. By the same token, five minutes of stretching your body can ground you and release anxiety or racing thoughts. Listening to uplifting music will also help you self-soothe, and going for a walk has benefits beyond exercise. As you learned in Chapter 1, the movements you make on a walk mimic those used during EMDR therapy to help patients recover from PTSD.

If you're lucky enough to have a trusted friend or family member, reach out to them, not to complain or gossip, but to share what you're feeling. You may have already experienced processing your thoughts and emotions out loud and feeling better and finding solutions as a result. The goal is not to solve all your problems

today, but to take baby steps toward getting your needs met. You
may have to overcome a lifetime of imprinting and that doesn't
happen overnight. It takes deep work and a commitment to yourself to change and starts with noticing nonjudgmentally the self-
sabotaging methods you use to self-soothe. What are some ways
you escape uncomfortable thoughts and emotions? For example,
I've used daydreaming, alcohol, and sugary foods. List them here:

1. _____

2. _____

3. _____

4. _____

5. _____

Next, think of how you've responded, or how you would
respond, to a close friend who's struggling with shame or inade-
quacy. Write down what you've done or said, or would do or say, in
such a situation.

_____

_____

Next, write down what you do or say to *yourself* in that same
situation. Is there a difference?

_____

_____

Commit to giving yourself the same grace you gave to your
friend in the first letter when you are suffering.

_____

_____

Incorporate meaningful self-compassion into your life by taking care of your needs instead of ignoring them or escaping through unhealthy coping mechanisms. That could mean taking five minutes to do some deep breathing. It could look like a new class or hobby, or scheduling dinner with a friend. Self-care looks different for each of us but needs to be a constant in all our lives. What's one form of self-compassion you'll give to yourself this week?

Look back at your list of unhealthy coping mechanisms. Next time you reach for one, whether it's a substance or a behavior, pay attention to what triggers you. What need or feeling are you trying to escape and how can you take care of that need instead of avoiding or minimizing it?

Make a new promise to stop and check in with yourself regularly instead of waiting until your body is crying out for help. Ask, *What do I need right now?* Then give that to yourself. It can be as simple as wrapping yourself in a hug, taking a deep breath, or making a cup of tea.

CHAPTER EIGHT

LEARNING TO RELAX

"Only when you are relaxed
can you see what's going on."

JANE CAMPION

WHEN I ASKED my client Siobhan what she did for fun, she replied that she liked to travel. When I asked how often she traveled, she said she had not taken a vacation in over two years. Instead of a hobby she engages in once or twice a week, she considered a rare travel experience her sole source of relaxation. It is not uncommon for adult children of dysfunctional families to list travel as their sole hobby or to have no hobbies at all. Relaxation and recreation for their own sake make them feel guilty and unproductive, even useless. For them, hobbies do not provide the pleasant distraction from life's hardships they do for most people. They become another obligation because they do not provide the sense of well-being and relief of tension they do for others.

Even travel may fall short as a source of relaxation if you've grown up in a dysfunctional home. A mind at rest can be so troubling that you create tension to simply feel alive. Bessel van der Kolk, author of *The Body Keeps the Score*, explains that survivors of childhood trauma only feel like themselves when they are in a traumatized state. When they are asked to rest their minds, they feel as though they cease to exist. That's why you may fill every moment of downtime with things to do that prevent you from having to face any empty space. Because of the way your brain has been rewired, simply "being" is not a viable option. Constant doing helps you feel safe and adequate, and ensures you do not have to face the intense discomfort of a mind with nothing to do.

Do you feel as though you can never relax, even on vacation? Is every spare moment filled with activities and obligations, many of which you don't even enjoy? It's possible you've subconsciously created this chaos as a maladaptive way to soothe yourself. Unfilled space leaves you restless and agitated or it makes you feel lazy and worthless. Most of all, it exposes you to unstructured time to reflect on yourself and your life and that can be too painful to face. As you may have guessed, the deep-seated reasons why you can never relax often track back to childhood. Here are five that may sound familiar to you.

1. Emotional neglect

Growing up, you received little praise or encouragement from your parents. As a result, you never experienced the pat on the back indicating you'd done well. You felt there was always more to do and nothing you did was good enough. That's why you fail to experience the grand exhale after a hard day's work. You never really feel like you're finished, and it's as though your off switch is broken. This leads to late nights binge-watching when you could be getting a good night's sleep. A part of you wants to take advantage of the time at night without responsibilities, but you sabotage yourself with lack of sleep and guilt over your inability to keep a normal bedtime.

2. You're afraid of being lazy

Growing up, you may have internalized a lot of faulty messaging around laziness. That messaging served the people around you very well. You may have been parentified and tasked with age-inappropriate responsibilities such as caring for younger siblings or preparing dinner. As a result, you can never relax because you're afraid of appearing lazy, even to yourself. You've been conditioned to serve, so you fill up your free time with obligations and taking care of others. It's possible you enjoy no free time at all. Between working a stressful job, caring for children at home, then rushing somewhere else to care for aging parents, there's no time for you.

3. You're overly responsible

As mentioned in the previous chapter, you already lack the basic fundamentals of self-care, having little idea of how to give yourself what you need. Add to that the reality that you lack the time to care for yourself due to your mountain of responsibilities. Even if you did experience downtime, you wouldn't know what to do with it. You've been trained since childhood to be overly responsible, so even though you have an idea you're doing more than your fair share, you don't know how to delegate to lighten your load. You may have a very real fear that things will fall apart, or someone may even die if you drop the ball.

Sadly, and often subconsciously, other people benefit from you tyrannizing yourself in this way. That's why they're not in a hurry to help you stop. It's up to you to gauge your own bandwidth and set the necessary boundaries to protect your health. Otherwise, you risk over-giving to the point of illness. Often, women develop auto-immune disease they don't realize is linked to stress and even that is not enough to make them stop. Gabor Maté writes about this phenomenon in his book *When the Body Says No.*

4. You grew up with conditional love

You received the message that love depended on your performance. If you got good grades or won athletic trophies or music competitions, then you would win your parents' approval. If you were a good little helper who never complained, then you might feel valued. You never felt loved for who you are, so you believe your value comes from your output. You have trouble understanding your intrinsic worth, and that you matter simply because you exist. Your worth has been fused in your mind to your productivity, so doing nothing or doing something just for fun makes you feel worthless. This is why childhood trauma survivors often lack hobbies or an outlet for their creativity. When someone asks you what you do for fun, do you have trouble coming up with a response? If, like Siobhan, you answer with "travel," remember that something you do once or twice a year does not qualify as an outlet, especially considering what we've discussed about our habits around so-called vacations.

5. You distract yourself

If your life feels inauthentic and unfulfilling, keeping busy distracts you from the fact that you're unhappy. It's a coping mechanism that prevents you from doing the hard work of changing. Time to yourself might leave you feeling empty because you have not cultivated an honest relationship with yourself. Self-connection is something you seek to escape rather than develop because deep down you feel unworthy of time to yourself. When you have space in your calendar, you rush to fill it with obligations to others because that prevents you from having to face the emptiness of time alone. Spending free time on yourself and things you enjoy makes you feel selfish, anyway, so you rush to help others, volunteer, or embark on another project rather than kick back and unwind.

Free time forces us to look at ourselves. That's when honest emotions creep in with all their inconvenient information. While a certain amount of distraction is healthy and that's where hobbies play a role, distracting ourselves from the reality of our emotions is not. If you've been conditioned to ignore your feelings, you're missing out on the rich fount of information they have to offer you. The anger you suppress is the catalyst for change you need. You fear anger because it got you punished or rejected or because you never learned to manage your emotions, so its power scares you. Mismanaged anger does have the power to do harm and you may have experienced that. However, healthy anger has the power to change your life for the better and is the emotion behind self-advocacy and solid boundaries. It is the feeling you have when you no longer tolerate treatment you've put up with for far too long.

If you're a person who can never relax, do any of the previous five items resonate with you? Are you willing to admit you can no longer go on this way and that choosing to continue will likely make you sick? Are you ready to break free from the conditioning that has kept you beholden to everyone but yourself? Most of all, do you desire a true connection with yourself and are you willing to take the necessary steps to do so? If you answer yes, take this as your challenge to stop filling your free time with activities that only serve to disconnect you from yourself and others, and learn the true meaning of what it means to relax.

Begin to face your fear of being alone or redefine what it means to spend time with yourself. Give up those late nights mindlessly watching, eating, or scrolling, and reserve space in your calendar just for you. Do what savvy entrepreneurs do and pay yourself first, but in time instead of money. Mark off space for you in your calendar *before* you fill it in with obligations to others. Instead of going shopping when you have extra time (a form of financial self-sabotage), spend that time mindfully journaling how you feel. Sit quietly for five or ten minutes and let your feelings arise. Here's the important part: don't judge them. Whatever thoughts or feelings come up, observe them uncritically. You'll be amazed at what a few minutes of quiet time will tell you about yourself and your life.

This may be the first time you've allowed yourself to have a thought or feeling without berating yourself or talking yourself out of it. How many times have you told yourself you shouldn't feel the way you do, other people have it harder, or this will pass? While the latter two may be true, they have no bearing on the first which is that you have every right to feel whatever way you do. When you talk yourself out of your feelings, you deny yourself the comfort we all deserve when we're feeling down. It contributes to your low self-worth because it is the ultimate form of self-betrayal and self-denial.

You may fear feeling overwhelmed by your feelings because you've never been taught to manage emotions. Suppressing them is not the answer and, as you've learned, doing so can harm your health. My experience sinking into my emotions instead of denying them has been that I do feel bad, sometimes very bad, but rarely longer than a day. And the self-discovery that results from an honest acceptance of my emotions is worth the pain. The pain of self-denial is far worse and longer lasting than the pain that comes when you acknowledge how you feel without judging yourself.

As Kristin Neff points out in her self-compassion research, you need not exaggerate your emotions or minimize them but take them as they come. You are not your feelings; you have feelings and as you observe them you will begin to understand the rich message they are trying to send you. Disconnecting from your emotions means denying yourself a fundamental aspect of who you are and that has led to the emptiness you've experienced. Allow yourself to fill that emptiness in ways that promote your personal growth instead of the old ways of coping that amount to harmful self-sabotage.

All your life, you've been discouraged from attending to your needs and instead made to focus on others, a lifelong conditioning that will take time to shift. You've been primed to ignore or suppress the signals your body gives that tell you when it's time to relax. Instead, you push through to exhaustion, and sitting still feels unbearable. In a counterintuitive way, self-neglect of this need for rest arose as a form of self-protection when you were a child. If any expression of a need got you punished, rejected, or abandoned, it would feel safer to not have any needs at all. Therefore, you minimized them, pushed them down, and did your best not to have them. Now, after a lifetime of ignoring them, you're supposed to magically know how to take care of them, but it doesn't work that way. That's why common advice around self-care is too simplistic for the complex PTSD survivor. It glosses over the deep and confounding reasons why such care eludes you and why you need to deal with that subconscious programming first.

When you've been forced to suppress your desires, true self-care starts with discovering what you want. This means getting out of your head and into your body. You may have trouble knowing what you want when you are asked to think about it. That's why it's called a heart's desire and not a head's desire. So, I encourage my clients to make a list of things they enjoy, using their senses as a guide. What sights, sounds, smells, touches, and tastes appeal to you? Write down twenty-five sensory delights, or as many as you can conjure up. Mine, for example, include the scent of lavender, the flavor of fine chocolate, and the feel of real silk on my skin.

Each day for the next week, commit to including at least one of these experiences into your day (the more, the better). My clients have found this simple exercise to be a profoundly moving experience that helps them connect with themselves in ways they never imagined. One woman I worked with posted an image of her fall décor to her social media page and received an overwhelming number of positive responses. Of course, the external validation is not what matters, but that it highlighted a hidden gift. Often, when we allow ourselves to spend time doing things we enjoy we discover talents that can even become marketable and create a stream of income. When you attend to your needs in this way, it improves all areas of your life, the same way neglecting those needs impacts all aspects of your life negatively.

Another way to connect with yourself is to set a timer for five or ten minutes and simply sit there. This mindful awareness means you pay attention to your thoughts and feelings without judging them. You may be surprised at the information you gain during these mindfulness sessions. The feelings you've suppressed have a chance to come to the surface and speak to you. You may feel tears come to your eyes, releasing the sadness that's stayed trapped in your body as you distracted yourself from your feelings. Since emotional avoidance can be unconscious, sitting still gives room for feelings you didn't know you had to make an appearance.

Mindful self-compassion has helped me come to terms with disappointment, an emotion I used to avoid like the plague. As a child, I had no one to comfort me through these feelings so I suppressed them. This became a subconscious conditioning that followed me around as an adult and prevented me from processing or even admitting to feeling let down. For most of us, even those who have not been traumatized, setbacks are a regular part of everyday life. Refusing to admit to disappointment meant disconnecting from an essential part of myself and denying myself comfort and compassion.

When someone or something disappointed me, I'd go straight into problem-solving mode, believing only I could make the situation better. This put more pressure on me and made me feel responsible for someone else dropping the ball. I would talk myself out of feeling let down by engaging in platitudes such as "things happen for a reason" or "other people have it worse." While these may be true, they are self-abandoning rather than self-compassionate. I needed to allow myself to feel disappointed and know it wasn't my fault and there was nothing I could have done differently to prevent the letdown. You may be so used to treating yourself this way, you don't see the cruelty of denying yourself the right to feel basic human emotions.

Instead of distracting yourself, tune into your body and ask, *What do you need right now?* Sometimes, I need to give myself a hug, a skill I only learned recently and that has been proven to have the same benefits as when someone else who loves you does the hugging. You really can give yourself the care you need, and the research now backs that up. A 2021 study by Aljoscha Dreisoerner et al. showed that when touch is unavailable from others, self-touch gestures provide an alternative way to reduce your strain. You may want to stop and pay attention to your surroundings as a grounding practice when you feel anxious. Using your senses as a guide again, point out things you can see, hear, smell, feel, and taste to remind yourself of your presence and safety in the here and now.

Our minds want to trick us into thinking we're never safe because of the way trauma gets stored in the body. Due to past trauma, your fight-or-flight system has been overactivated and has trouble shutting down. You may notice that you overreact to loud noises or surprises and struggle to return your nervous system to baseline. Also called the sympathetic nervous system, activation of the fight-or-flight mechanism *de-activates* the parasympathetic nervous system, which helps us "rest and digest." You find it hard to relax because of the constant engagement of your fight-or-flight response, which prevents your body from enjoying the safety essential to rest and relaxation.

You can provide yourself comfort and soothing in many simple ways. If you begin to feel overwhelmed stop and set a timer for five minutes and pay attention to your breath. This small mindfulness practice works wonders to reset your nervous system. You may also choose to do a vagus nerve reset, which can help you process and release stress stored in your body and involves a few simple exercises, mostly above the neck. Going for a walk will also help you slow down the hamster wheel in your mind so you can relax and find peace.

Mindfulness meditation can help relieve the anxiety that arises as a natural outcome of this overactive fight-or-flight response. You can search examples on YouTube or simply set a timer and watch your thoughts and feelings go by without judgment. You may practice for as little as three or up to twenty minutes or more. The research shows you will experience benefits in as little as four days, and it's better to practice shorter sessions more frequently than longer sessions sporadically. You may choose to focus on your breath at first and then open up to whatever arises as the practice goes on. By attending to your thoughts and feelings, you increase self-connection and your ability to relax as you learn that you need do nothing to "succeed" at meditation. Your practice becomes a metaphor for your life as you stop striving and trying so hard and simply accept where you are right now.

There's a reason why you might feel more empty after a spa day (not to mention depleted financially). When you tune into your body's needs, you find that it rarely says it needs a manicure or facial. The common practices that come to mind when we think of the phrase *self-care* may not apply to the complex PTSD survivor. Because of what happened to you, your body lacks a basic feeling of safety. You may in fact be overreaching when you go to fancy salons and spas to get your fix. A hand on your heart or a deep conscious breath may go further than all the pampering in the world toward helping you feel more regulated. And it is from this place of regulation and peace that we make better decisions that impact the rest of our lives.

CHAPTER NINE

STOPPING SELF-IMPOSED ISOLATION

> "If you want to end your isolation, you must be honest about what you want at a core level and decide to go after it."
>
> MARTHA BECK

WE'RE LIVING IN A TIME when isolation has become more common. Even before the pandemic that started in 2020, people reported higher levels of loneliness and less in-person interaction. For some, however, isolation is a self-imposed state brought on by fear of interacting with others. That could be due to pain from past experience, or the feeling that it's just easier to be alone. This is not an introvert/extrovert distinction: though introverts may crave more alone time, they are often better at cultivating deep, connected relationships. They do not isolate out of fear and pain unless there are other factors at play.

Those other factors could involve unresolved childhood trauma. Chronic feelings of loneliness and a tendency to avoid social interactions have been linked to adverse events in childhood. If you find yourself needing more and more time alone or feeling lonelier among others than you do by yourself, unmet childhood needs could be the culprit. If you felt forced to suppress your needs to win the love and acceptance of your caregivers, you never felt celebrated for your authentic self. You had to play a role to maintain your membership in the group, and now you believe that requirement extends to all groups. So, in social situations you wear a mask that displays a false self while your true self stays hidden even from yourself. Of course, playing this part becomes exhausting after a time and that's why you decide it's easier to be alone.

Following you'll find five reasons why your unmet childhood needs impact your ability or willingness to connect in adulthood. See how many resonate with you.

---

1. People trigger you

You might decide it's easier to be on your own because of how other people trigger you or set your nervous system on edge. If you grew up without learning how to handle your emotions or resolve conflict, dealing with others can feel like walking through a field of land mines. It's not people you're avoiding, but your own reaction to what they might say or do. You can't predict how others are going to behave and can easily become dysregulated by a comment or opinion. That's because as a child you were forced to suppress your honest thoughts and feelings and now as an adult you tend to silence or censor yourself. Subconsciously, however, you blame the other person for your own inability to voice your opinions. You feel angry at them for having the privilege to speak their mind when you won't allow yourself to do the same.

Have you ever noticed yourself feeling resentful of others for displaying behavior that you suppress? For example, I felt contempt for women who cried in public and continued talking through their tears. To me, that felt as disgusting as watching someone throw up. I understand now how that disdain for honest emotion related to my own inability to share my feelings with others. I had numbed myself as a self-protective measure because no one comforted me through my emotions or helped me process them. I viewed emotions as a sign of weakness. As you recall from the discussion in Chapter 2 about attachment styles, emotional neglect makes you believe your emotions push people away rather than create connection. I projected my own rejection of my emotions onto others and refused them the compassion and freedom to feel that I had refused myself.

The many ways people trigger you feel random and outside your control. If the situation involves drinking alcohol, like at a party, that lowered inhibition may make you say things you regret. Under the influence, you have less of the discipline it takes to act as a dam against the tsunami of emotions you've been suppressing your whole life. That's why being around others is neither relaxing nor comforting, but challenging and counterproductive. It feels easier to be on your own where you can rest safe in the knowledge that nothing and no one will "trip you up." In my recovery program, one of the reasons people gave for drinking alone is so they would stop hurting people.

2. You have poor boundaries

If you grew up in a home where you learned your needs don't matter, you'll develop poor boundaries because no one taught you the importance of setting limits, standing up for yourself, or having your needs met. In fact, many families teach the opposite. You learned to suppress your emotions, pretend to be okay, and never ask for help, which makes it difficult to cultivate authentic and connected relationships. You believe you have to earn love and acceptance and the only way to do so is to abandon yourself and give to others. That leaves little incentive to get involved in relationships. "What's in it for me?" you might rightly ask.

For you, relationships lack the give-and-take that characterize healthy connections. Since you believe emotions push people away or make them leave, you will hold your feelings close to your vest in a misguided effort to preserve the relationship. You may never have learned that when others open up to you that's an invitation to open up to them in return. As a result, you take the listening position or change the subject when things get too deep. You may feel unable to enter into the intimacy required to form authentic friendships. You are too busy people-pleasing and over-giving to establish your own wants and needs in the relationship. Healthy people will sense the dishonesty and lack of depth in their interactions with you and keep their distance—affirming your fear of rejection. Unhealthy people are all too happy to take advantage of your lack of good boundaries and that's why you find yourself surrounded by them. Such people exhaust and deplete you to the point that you decide it's better to be alone.

3. Attachment issues

As we learned in Chapter 2, unmet childhood needs cause insecure attachment. When your parents fail to bond with you properly, you'll have trouble bonding with others, not to mention yourself. Instead of finding ways to meet your own needs, you'll double down on getting them met in your adult relationships by transferring your desire for love, acceptance, and understanding from your parents to your peers. You learn over and over that another person will never make up for your parents' failures, but you can't stop looking to others to validate you.

Without any idea how to get your needs met honestly, you continue to experience the frustration your parents caused with their neglect. So, hurt and disappointment become the familiar refrain of every relationship you enter into, which makes you withdraw to avoid the recurring pain. You gravitate toward people who will never see you or meet your need for love and acceptance because they remind you of "home." For example, a woman with a distant father will find herself attracted to emotionally unavailable men. She may find nice men who want to treat her well "boring" or even repulsive, ensuring she continues the cycle of abuse and neglect until she decides relationships are too painful and goes into isolation instead.

4. Weak sense of self

Healthy parents help their children understand who they are and develop their strengths. They give them continual feedback and offer praise and encouragement. They hold a mirror up to their children that tells them who they are and what they're good at. This guides their journey in life and helps them decide which path to pursue, be it in education, relationships, or career. If, on the other hand, your parents ignored you in childhood and made you feel like a burden, you will develop a weak sense of self and a poor self-image. You will lack the road map to life as you struggle to understand your likes and dislikes or what you're good at because the most important adults in your life failed to offer you any guidance.

Without a strong sense of self, you will lack the core values that help you choose the right people to connect with. These are the morals and principles you follow that guide you like a compass toward the most authentic and fulfilling life for you. Without core values to guide you, you are tossed to and fro depending on what other people want from you at the time. Instead of making decisions from a strong internal sense of right and wrong or what's best for you, you have an external focus that sees you making decisions based on other people's values or needs. This is why you choose relationships in which your needs go unmet, and you might have the feeling you're living someone else's life. You may begin to believe you have a "broken picker" and mistrust your own instincts when it comes to judging character. Your desire to isolate increases as you feel other people only hurt and disappoint you, and you're baffled as to how to pick the ones who won't.

5. Social anxiety

Suffering through parental abuse or neglect crushes a child's confidence. Combined with a poor sense of self, that low confidence makes social interactions fraught with difficulty. You anticipate rejection because you received so much of it. As a result, you tend to view neutral expressions as disapproving and clamor to put a smile on people's faces. That approval you never received from your parents you try desperately to get from others. As a child, you were never sure what you needed to do to win acceptance, so you default to over-giving, agreeableness, and people-pleasing.

Instead of showing up as yourself (because you're not sure who that is), you try to become what you think others want. This backfires as healthy people will sense something is "off" and give you wide berth. This only breaks your heart again and confirms your deepest suspicions that you're unlovable. It may be hard to hear that your attempts at people-pleasing come off as deceitful to healthy acquaintances, but it's a fact that a failure to communicate your boundaries is a form of dishonesty. You may want to review Chapter 4 as a reminder that healthy people want you to express your needs and emotions, not kowtow to theirs.

The common self-help advice for social anxiety is exposure therapy, but exposing yourself to scary situations requires a certain level of safety before it can help us. You need to be mindful of your window of tolerance and the fact your past trauma may have narrowed yours. The window of tolerance refers to the ideal emotional state for optimal functioning. If you're outside your window, you're either hyper-aroused, which feels like anxiety or overwhelm, or hypo-aroused, which means feeling numbed out or depressed. As a survivor of childhood trauma, you more easily move into these suboptimal states of arousal—and have more trouble returning to "normal." Your window of tolerance has shrunk due to what you've been through, and you struggle to function effectively as a result. This may help explain why life feels hard and you have trouble with tasks and situations that others sail through.

When you're operating outside your window of tolerance, it's a form of "white knuckling" or getting through by the skin of your teeth. When exposing yourself to social situations without regulating your nervous system, each interaction seems worse than the last and confirms your fears rather than alleviates them. Fed up with repeated humiliation, you settle for a life of isolation. The loneliness of someone who's experienced childhood trauma is different than situational loneliness because it's chronic. Rather than external forces like a pandemic, the social isolation of the person who suffers from adverse childhood experiences (ACEs) comes from within.

The key elements of this type of social isolation are shame and feeling less than. You feel ashamed for not putting yourself out there, but when you do go out, you experience social anxiety from feeling not good enough. That makes you behave in ways that can repel people, like wearing a mask or fawning to win acceptance. You anticipate rejection and use counterproductive methods to try to avoid it, and the shame spiral continues; your fears become self-fulfilling prophecies, and you self-isolate once again. So, how do you get out of the damaging cycle and enter life fully engaged and open?

1. Acknowledge your loneliness

Growing up, you learned to suppress your emotions, so simply acknowledging them can feel foreign. Instead of giving yourself compassion over how you feel, you criticize yourself for feeling that way. Shame about your social isolation overrides the primary feeling of loneliness, so rather than caring for your primary feeling, you pour shame on top and deal with that instead. Shame only makes you want to hide and prevents you from reaching out to others.

2. Remember, you're not alone

It's easy to tell yourself you're the only one who struggles with social isolation, but loneliness is on the rise for everyone. Even before the pandemic, people reported a decrease in loving relationships. See yourself as part of a larger whole, filled with many others who feel exactly as you do. You are part of a community of people recovering from childhood trauma and you belong to the larger community of those who may be experiencing deep loneliness for the first time. As you'll remember from Chapter 7, this common humanity is the second pillar of self-compassion. It helps to know that others share your suffering, and it stops the counterproductive approach of denying you have any suffering to begin with.

3. Reach out

It takes courage to change, and that means reaching out to someone you trust. Tell them the truth about how you feel instead of pretending you're okay. Pay attention to the ways you may resist this type of intimacy. I remember friends opening up to me and feeling so uncomfortable that I'd change the subject or minimize their plight. I missed an opportunity to deepen the friendship and the invitation to share my own inner world. If you have no one you can safely share with, consider talking with a therapist, or joining a group online with whom you can unpack your feelings anonymously.

4. Get out each day

The movement of walking and being outside in nature serves as a balm for your mental health and improves your mood. If you live in an area where you can mingle with strangers, interact with someone in a low-stakes way like petting their dog. You might set goals for yourself, like speaking to one stranger every day. It could be as simple as making a friendly comment to someone in line at the store. If you're not ready to interact, walking among people may also help you feel less alone (especially if you keep in mind the principle of common humanity). Lovingkindness meditation may also help increase your connection to yourself and others as it involves repeating phrases that remind you of the give-and-take in loving relationships.

5. Journal

Take time to journal your thoughts and feelings: writing for even ten minutes in free flow about your emotions can yield surprising results. It will bring you closer to understanding yourself and what you really want. If your parents never gave you feedback or encouragement, it's now up to you to discern who you are, your likes and dislikes, desires, and goals. Getting to know yourself will prevent you from abandoning your needs because you will begin to make decisions based on your values instead of what you think others want from you.

6. Set boundaries

Practice setting boundaries with others rather than avoiding them. If you tend to let other people do all the talking, for example, make a commitment to volunteer more information about yourself.

Counter opinions with which you disagree rather than remaining silent. Expressing yourself means sharing your thoughts rather than pretending you agree to avoid conflict. If the person gets upset, that's pertinent information to help you decide if you want to further engage with them. You can either change the subject or extract yourself from this one-sided conversation with someone who struggles to respect views different from their own. You're not obligated to act as a sounding board for someone who thinks conversations should only go one way. Remind yourself that your needs matter, too, and it's your job to protect them.

7. Take baby steps to combat social isolation

We've learned that throwing yourself into social situations over and over again may not be the best way to beat social isolation. The common belief that the more you do it, the more comfortable you will feel, has been proven false. While this type of exposure may work for some, it backfires on someone whose social isolation stems from childhood trauma. Instead of enhancing your social skills, you may experience multiple rejections and failures that make you ever more fearful of putting yourself out there.

Rather than plugging your nose and jumping in the deep end, put a toe in the water. Start with the lower-risk interactions mentioned above and give yourself credit for courage rather than performance. Remain conscious of your needs, especially physical ones, throughout every interaction. Do you need to take a deep breath or give yourself a loving touch to stay connected? These self-regulating strategies can be done without anyone noticing. You can also excuse yourself to the bathroom and enclose yourself in a full embrace.

You are so used to externalizing your focus to others that turning your gaze within will feel like a shift. Practice tuning into yourself first as you connect with the person in front of you. Pay attention to the pace of your speech and take the time you need to speak your piece. You might rush through because, as a child, adults placed little value on what you had to say, but that's no longer the case. You deserve to feel seen and heard as much as anyone else. It is your right to take up space and make your thoughts and feelings known so that others can get to know the real you. Wearing a mask will only prevent the connection you crave. The old advice about listening more than you speak to win friends and influence people has been debunked. The most current research shows that those who talk slightly more than they listen come across as more likeable. And, although popularity is not the goal, understanding that incessant listening does nothing to improve your image may help you curb the habit.

You may have taken pride in your role as a good listener. Society encourages you with adages like "You were born with one mouth and two ears for a reason." It's true that authentic listening is a wonderful quality and there's not enough of it in our world. People rush in with platitudes or empty words when all you need is someone to hear you and acknowledge your feelings. However, inauthentic listening has the aim of people-pleasing and prevents you from sharing your own thoughts and feelings. It comes from a place of fear of being seen and known for who you are. It attracts people who will take advantage of your willingness to enter into and sustain a one-sided conversation that only benefits them. Healthy conversation requires a somewhat equal amount of talking and listening. Over the course of a relationship, there will be times when you do more listening than talking and vice versa, but overall, these should be fairly equal.

CHAPTER TEN

HEALING LOVE ADDICTION

"Like an addiction to alcohol and other drugs, a dependency on love begins to feel like an unstable state in which a person begins to lose herself to the experience."

BRENDA SCHAEFFER

IN 1985, *Women Who Love Too Much* by Robin Norwood took the world by storm. The book told countless stories of women who stood by men whose love fell far out of reach. Women (and men) who love too much share the trait of self-abandonment: instead of asking for what they want, they twist themselves to fit into what someone else wants or needs. Much of the self-improvement taught by dating coaches revolves around adopting qualities that romantic prospects find desirable rather than tuning into what you want and need. It's another form of externalizing and turning the gaze outward for cues on how to behave. It plays into all the false beliefs you may have adopted around what you must do to receive love and acceptance. It makes love feel like something hard to get or that you have to work toward strategically and even manipulatively.

You know from experience that trying to earn love hasn't worked. The more you strove to win your parents' love and affection, the more remote they might have seemed. However, this model feels like home to you and results in you subconsciously creating the same dynamics with your partners. Some say you are trying to re-create the same pattern so that you can get it right this time. However, without the knowledge of what you're doing wrong and with advice that tacitly encourages you to keep abandoning yourself, it's difficult to break the pattern. Like your parents, romantic interests who require you to do all the work are never going to give you what you need, anyway.

Susan Peabody wrote about the phenomenon in her book *Addiction to Love*, so-called because the obsessive relationships she describes seem impossible to extricate from. Love addiction is different from sex addiction and affects women more than men. The most common reason for this behavior is childhood emotional neglect and abuse. Due to a poor sense of self, love addicts look to someone else to "complete" them. They believe this person will solve all their problems and make life worth living. One key feature of love addiction involves the creation of fantasy relationships.

You may be familiar with the feeling of intense interest in someone who shows little interest in you. Or perhaps you were lured in by someone's early devotion to you, only to discover he was after sex and nothing more. You may remember skipping over the getting-to-know-you phase and propelling yourself into a future that includes marriage and undying devotion. However, this future exists only in your mind because the object of your desire has shown no sign with either words or actions that he feels the same way. In fact, he may have given you clues of the exact opposite—that he has no intention of sharing a future with you. These maladaptive and self-damaging mind patterns echo a childhood in which you had to convince yourself your parents cared and would do anything to protect you, even when they demonstrated no such intention. Here are seven signs you suffer from love addiction; see how many resonate with you.

1. You are drawn to unavailable people

These partners are either physically or emotionally unavailable for a meaningful relationship. They could be married or have an addiction they prioritize over you, whether that's work or a substance or pornography. They might have narcissistic qualities, avoid intimacy, or simply show no interest in a deeper relationship with you. They likely have their own unresolved issues from childhood that make them unable to form close attachments. They fear intimacy in the same way you do. Yes, choosing unavailable partners is a subconscious way to avoid a true connection with someone.

If deep down, you are scared of being seen and known for who you really are, you will choose people who pose no threat to that fear of exposure. At the same time, you can fool yourself into thinking it's their fault you don't have a more connected relationship. That's how your subconscious mind keeps the painful cycle of unmet needs in relationships and avoids the possibility of growth and intimacy. You create a fantasy relationship because it's easier than facing the reality that this person is not interested. That means you invent a relationship in your mind that's nothing like the real one and ignore all the red flags that tell you this person is unsafe and wrong for you. Instead, you cling to your plans for the future, including marriage, but the object of your affection shows no signs the relationship is going anywhere.

2. You find nice people boring

It's impossible for you to feel attracted to people who are nice and treat you well. You find a way to sabotage any chance of relationship with them because they are not creating the chaos you crave. Although painful, you need the internal turmoil provoked by an unavailable partner. You mistake the insecurity and poor treatment for passion because love has always felt difficult and hurtful to you, and a kind partner will not feel like "home." This is why we must not mistake that instant chemical attraction for a green light. In fact, it may be the red flag saying you're about to enter into a danger zone, so beware.

3. You compromise your values

In an effort to win love, you keep moving your boundaries, if you had any to begin with. You make excuses for poor behavior and take up with an addict, for instance, even though you said you never would. You may struggle to set standards for yourself because deep down you don't believe you deserve to have them met. Or perhaps part of you believes no one will meet them so you may as well lower them to be realistic. Love addiction makes you elevate the other person so that you cater to their needs more than your own. You'll abandon yourself to keep this person interested, and try to fit yourself into the relationship rather than asking if this person's right for you. You may even use sex to get or keep attention, even when that's not what you really want.

As a child you became accustomed to not receiving what you wanted and having to settle for what someone was willing to give you. Most of the time that wasn't much. Now, this is different from the parent who simply lacks the resources and wishes they could give you more. I'm referring to the intangible assets of attention, security, love, and respect. As a result, instead of feeling intrinsically valued, you looked outside yourself for signs of your worthiness. Rather than getting clear on your values and using them as a guide on your relationship journey, you find out what the other person wants so you can give it to them. You falsely believe this is the way to get your needs met—even though it's never worked in the past.

4. You think if you try hard enough, you'll win love

To you, red flags are less danger signs than temporary obstacles to overcome. You think with enough love and understanding you'll coax this person into a relationship, even when there is a pattern of evading commitment. You cling to a fantasy that you're the one who will get through. You approach relationships with the same striving you did with your parents or caregivers—striving that never got your needs met, by the way, and which will have the same result today. You feel that it is up to you to make things work while the other person gets let off the hook. This is the conditioning your parents instilled in you to assuage any guilt they may have felt about failing to meet your needs.

5. You're obsessed with thoughts of the person

When you're with friends, this person is all you talk about. You're constantly checking your phone to see if your beloved has texted or called. You suffer the ongoing pain of insecurity due to the power imbalance of caring more than the other person. You think about the person continually to the detriment of other activities. You feel unfocused at work, for example, as you daydream about your future or check your phone for texts. Your obsession makes you compromise other relationships as you decline invitations or cancel dates with friends because you want to make yourself available.

6. You believe a relationship will rescue you

Even if someone all but ignores you, you believe this person is the one who can solve all your problems. You're convinced he or she will make your life perfect if only you can uncover the "real" person inside. You tell yourself that once that happens, this person will understand you were meant for each other, and you can finally feel complete. If you only need less and give more, he or she will become your savior and fulfill the empty space inside.

7. You re-create past trauma

You're attracted to partners who hurt you the same way your parents did in childhood. You reenact this desperate need to win their love by becoming clingy and frantic for their attention (symptoms of anxious attachment style). This activates the person's fear of intimacy, and they pull away, which only makes you work harder to win their affection. This dynamic is sometimes called a *trauma bond* which refers to a relationship characterized by unhealthy feelings or even abuse, but one you cannot tear yourself away from. The feeling of longing for someone who appears distant or as though he cares much less about you is compelling because it's familiar. It triggers the same false promise it did with your mom or dad (or another caregiver): *if I only try hard enough, this person will love me; if I can only be perfect, this person will finally see I'm worthwhile.*

As with our parents, we hold ourselves to an unattainable standard of perfection but apply no standard at all to the object of our affection. You second-guess your actions and replay conversations in your mind for what you could have done differently. All this feeds into the fantasy that there is some magical way to reach this person if you can only discover it. Instead of taking someone's behavior as indications that they are not relationship ready, you take them as challenges to overcome. That's how your little inner child survived similar neglect from your parents.

It's too scary for a child to believe their parents are unloving, so you told yourself you must be doing something wrong. It's *your* fault that someone else is behaving badly toward you. Do you hear the ridiculousness of this statement? But you have been telling yourself this for years. That's how dating can play into and trigger your traumatic experience. You set poor boundaries in relationships because your parents have conditioned you to believe you alone are responsible for keeping a relationship alive.

What Causes Love Addiction?

Women and men who love too much seek the love they never received as children. Your father or mother's affection felt out of reach. So, you re-enact that childhood drama by yearning for, and never receiving, love from someone else. Instead of learning from experience and leaving one-sided relationships, you double down.

Either with the same person or another unavailable partner, you keep pursuing those who will never return your love. As in childhood, you assume the problem lies with you. If only you were more understanding, prettier, more perfect, you'd win love. It's a trick now as it was then and keeps you from ever having your needs met.

Although your conscious mind tells you otherwise, you do not want a real relationship. You may want to read that again. You pursue these hopeless cases because they protect you from your deep fear of intimacy, an intimacy you've been trained to do without if you want to stay in your parents' good graces. In addition, if you never received the love and affection you needed, you will feel unworthy of love and subconsciously take steps to avoid receiving it. This harmful form of self-sabotage manifests in artificial relationships with people who will never give you what you say you want.

Your unconscious avoidance of being seen and known may originate from your unclear sense of self. Or you may have a deep-seated fear that there is something wrong with you, which stems from your parents' lack of love and acceptance. In your mind, if anyone really knew you, they wouldn't like you, so you get involved with people who have no interest in knowing you. This keeps you safe from the exposure you dread. At the same time, you tell yourself that making this person fall in love with you will solve all your problems. It's a maladaptive mindset that ensures you stay frustrated and unfulfilled in your romantic life without understanding why. Not only will this person never fall in love with you, but another person is also not the answer to your internal emptiness. You need to get to the root of your false self-impressions that result in self-loathing and self-sabotage. This means resolving your past and understanding who you are and what you really want and need.

How to Recover from Love Addiction

Take Time Alone for Self-Care

Love addicts often go from one relationship to another without time in between to assess what went wrong or how to grow from the experience. This is another symptom of the anxious attachment style. Take time alone to date yourself for a while. Taking care of your needs will help you value yourself more. As your self-worth increases, you'll feel less needy and desperate for someone else to fulfill you. Just as we need self-connection before we can connect with others, self-fulfillment comes from within rather than as a product of what others give us.

Establish Values

In Chapter 4, you took the time to establish your core values. These will help you get to know yourself better and decide what you will and won't tolerate. Your values give you a clearer view of the type of partner that will add to your life because they tell you what matters to you most. Values serve as a compass that guides you on the road of life. They help you make decisions that ensure you are heading in the direction of the most authentic and fulfilling experience you can have with your limited time on planet Earth. Learning yours and getting to know them intimately will help you make better choices when it comes to partners.

See Dating as Information-Gathering

If you struggle with love addiction, you may treat dating as a one-sided test where you prove your worthiness as a romantic partner. You feel as though every first date is with "the one" and endure crushing disappointment when that turns out to be untrue. Begin to see dating instead as an information-gathering exercise. That does not mean you turn dates into interviews. However, listen to what this person is telling you without sugar-coating it or telling yourself it means something different. Ask for clarification if you need to but otherwise take the words at face value. If someone says "I don't believe in marriage," and you want to get married someday, don't assume you'll change your date's mind. Take it as a sign this is probably not the right pick for you because you don't share the same values.

Understand Love Addiction

Read *Women Who Love Too Much* by Robin Norwood or *Addiction to Love* by Susan Peabody to help you understand your obsessive compulsion. You'll see you're not alone and there is hope for recovery. Love addicts often have another addiction that needs to be dealt with before the love addiction can be overcome. When I went into recovery from alcohol abuse, I remember my horror at discovering my twelve-step sponsor expected me to refrain from relationships for at least a year. In my mind, men were the distraction I counted on to get me through life without alcohol. However, the chaos and pain I would have encountered in relationships at that early stage of recovery would have sent me straight back to the bottle. In fact, I had never interacted with a romantic interest without a drink—or several.

That year away from men helped me see how I'd suffered with love addiction in my past. Wanting to skip the initial phases of dating to get to the life partner stage reflected my fear of being seen because I didn't know who I was. I believed subconsciously that if someone knew the real me, they wouldn't like it and would leave. So, I presented myself in a certain way to capture their attention, which is, of course, unsustainable. Eventually, they would see how insecure and needy I really was. They would find out I had trouble understanding and regulating my emotions or communicating in an honest, healthy way.

Insecurity is not something you need to hide, but if you attract unhealthy avoidant partners like I did, they won't know how to deal with it. Anxious and avoidant attachment types tend to gravitate to each other, and if they're not aware of their needs they can cause each other a lot of pain. A securely attached person, however, can help an anxious type become more secure. The key is to be honest about what you need and willing to work on things with your partner and possibly a mental health professional. Of course, I did nothing close to that sort of self-care and was too busy trying to hide my real self and present an image that would get me liked and wanted.

Now I view dating as a personal growth exercise. Each encounter helps me better understand myself and what I want—and don't want—in a relationship partner. Setting standards and sticking with them builds the self-worth muscle that had atrophied from underuse. I've shifted my perspective from asking what they want to asking myself the same question. It's scary to set boundaries because you fear you might lose someone, but that's the whole point of boundaries. If someone exits because of a boundary you've set, that's a reason to celebrate. Both because you've weeded out a poor prospect, and because you've had the courage to stand up for yourself and what you want.

Popular culture makes falling in love sound like mental illness, referring to it as being crazy about someone. Indeed, the early phases of romantic engagement come with a flood of chemicals that can throw you off-kilter. With that kind of PR, it's easy to believe passion equals chaos, but love should not be crazy making. It is possible to have a love relationship without feeling the pain and insecurity of not knowing where you stand. You can enjoy love without abandoning yourself or pretending to be something you're not. You will share relationships with people who see and hear you and want to know your needs so they can help you fulfill them. Most importantly, you'll learn that no one person can fulfill all your needs or make your life worth living. Only you can do that.

CHAPTER ELEVEN

LETTING GO OF ESCAPE FANTASIES

"Most of us have two lives: the life we
live and the unlived life within us."

STEVEN PRESSFIELD

MANY PEOPLE who experienced childhood trauma learn to avoid painful feelings by escaping into fantasies or intense daydreaming. I remember looking out the window during car rides and getting lost in the clouds, not saying a word, totally detached from the reality of the vehicle and my family within it. My parents would comment on how quiet it was back there, but silence felt like the only way to avoid their criticism, contempt, or rejection. I didn't realize it at the time, but my reality was too painful to bear, so I escaped into daydreaming instead. As I grew older, that daydreaming intensified to the point that I'd create scenarios in my mind with me as the star player. Unlike my role in real life as the invisible girl, only noticed to be maligned or criticized, I became powerful and popular. The scenarios changed, but the intent of the daydreaming remained the same: to remove me from my intolerable reality and into one where I felt seen, understood, loved, and respected.

In these escape fantasies, which started around age twelve, I credited my devoted parents with helping me reach heights as a celebrity in whatever field I'd decided to concoct that day. I could spend hours in these daydreams and, though they did not hold me back from completing daily tasks, their impact on my psyche proved far more insidious. They prevented me from pursuing my real dreams because it became too easy to drift into a fantasy where they had already been fulfilled and then some. As an adult and a writer, I had published articles and essays across numerous publications, but a book-length work felt out of my reach. On a subconscious level I knew my daydreaming would prevent me from committing to the focus required for such a long-term task.

My daydreaming shared the symptoms of my alcoholism—I wanted to stop but could not. Unlike the alcohol addiction I had overcome, no support group existed for people whose daydreams took over their lives (or so I thought). Believing myself to be the only person in the world who struggled with such an issue, I kept it to myself, which did nothing to solve the problem. Anything could trigger my fantasizing, including music of almost any kind and movie scenes. Avoiding all the triggers felt impossible and I experienced the same confusion over my inability to stop as I did with my drinking. One day, desperate to find some way to control this habit that threatened to take over my life, I googled it.

To my amazement, entries popped up, filled with stories from other people who struggled with the exact same issue as me. Their scenarios may have differed, but the principle remained the same. Like me, these people lost many of their waking hours in intense daydreams that offered an escape from reality. Aware of their actions but incapable of stopping, the compulsion mirrored any other addiction in which short-term pleasure wins out over long-term pain. Some of them had consulted with psychologists who mistakenly believed they suffered with disassociation. Or they minimized the habit as the typical daydreaming everyone does, which offers a healthy distraction from everyday life.

It's true that everyone daydreams but not for hours on end and not to the detriment of their career, relationship, and other life goals. As I went down the rabbit hole of the Internet, I came to understand that a psychologist in Israel, Dr. Eli Somer, had coined a term for the affliction in 2002 and begun to research the phenomenon: *maladaptive daydreaming (MD)*. That's the name for the condition in which you create a fantastic inner world complete with storylines and recurring characters. It's an idealized world where the daydreamer feels accepted, loved, admired, and respected, in stark contrast to their earthly experience. It's a way to get your emotional needs met when they aren't met in real life, but of course, your actual needs won't get addressed inside your head. Escaping into manufactured worlds holds you back from fulfilling your potential in life. According to Somer, studies show a correlation between childhood trauma and MD, but that is not the only factor at play. Twenty percent of MD sufferers also have an ADHD diagnosis, and there's a higher prevalence of the condition in young adults and children.

Like many competent psychologists, Dr. Somer learned from listening to his patients. He discovered that this form of daydreaming differed from both the "normal" and the dissociative. He understood the compulsion to daydream came from the intense pleasure derived from the experience, one that operated at the level of an addiction and that could not be overcome without treatment. With maladaptive daydreaming, you know you're doing it but can't make yourself stop. It's often accompanied by movement and triggered by music. Like many addictions, the experience feels intensely pleasurable at the time but is followed by equally intense shame and the real-life impact of sabotage on many aspects of your life. When all your emotional needs get met within the daydream, it takes away the incentive to work on those things in your life. This is not the same as dissociation because you're aware you're doing it, but it can prevent you from moving forward or making changes in life to improve your situation.

Have you had the experience of puzzling over something alone your whole life and then getting your answer within minutes? That's how I felt when I googled my condition. This is one example of why isolating rarely helps us solve our problems and keeps us stuck in the same patterns no matter how hard we try to change them. Although it can be useful to get alone and quiet (with God, if you're a person of faith), you need the insight of others who might know more about the subject or who simply let you know you're not alone. You may have been trained since childhood to go it alone and that served you as a survival mechanism back then. As an adult, however, you must retrain yourself to seek the help of others, not only for connection, but to make progress on your goals and dreams—progress that's impossible in a vacuum.

Ironically, Somer had submitted his findings to his peers in the research community and they did psychology's version of laughing him out of the room. He, too, found validation for his work online from the people he set out to help: people who suffered with maladaptive daydreaming. He developed a treatment program for MD, which utilized the MBSR (mindfulness-based stress reduction) model developed by Jon Kabat-Zinn in the 1970s, which had seen success treating chronic pain, anxiety, and depression. Mindfulness means paying attention to the present moment without judgment. Instead of dwelling on the past or fretting over the future, you ground yourself in this moment in time.

When you hear the term mindfulness, meditation probably comes to mind. You might think of sitting still for a set amount of time and focusing on your breath or trying to clear your mind of all thoughts. While that is one way to stay present, mindfulness can also be practiced in simple everyday activities, like exercise. By focusing on your movements instead of your thoughts, you calm the fretfulness that arises when your mind starts racing with fears about the future or regret over the past. Mindfulness can also mean taking in your surroundings. Focusing on what you see, touch, and smell in this moment. Grounding exercises like inhaling the scent of an essential oil or stroking a chenille blanket help relieve anxious thoughts and remind you that you are safe right here, right now.

Somer invited those struggling with MD to take part in the self-directed eight-week program online in which they practiced things like mindful eating, body scans, mindful walking, and journaling MD triggers. He instructed them to pay attention to their maladaptive daydreaming sessions without judging or criticizing them or trying to stop. He never gave them goals to reach for reducing their daydreaming and encouraged them not to go "cold turkey." Daydreaming for a short time (thirty minutes) could even be used as a reward after all daily tasks were completed. This would ensure the daydreaming did not get in the way of what they wanted to achieve in life. Somer expressed admiration for the creative minds of those struggling with the condition and praised the ability to create such profound happiness using only one's own mind. His outlook highlights how the creative gift of MD could be channeled into real-life pursuits and reap excellent rewards.

After eight sessions and a six-month follow-up, Somer's program was seen to have a significant effect, with many participants no longer meeting the diagnostic criteria for maladaptive daydreaming. The program's success in helping sufferers reduce MD through mindfulness reinforces the truth of the power of self-compassion versus self-criticism to garner results. The world often spreads the belief that shame is a positive catalyst for good behavior. As a result, you may have believed being hard on yourself would help you do better. However, shame does nothing but force you to go underground and isolate with your condition, which only ensures you never get the help you need to change.

The well-worn expression "What you resist persists" rings true. Staying present and getting curious about their MD rather than running from it or letting it have its way with them produced positive change in the study's participants. The powerlessness they felt over their compulsion to daydream transformed into something more manageable with no "willpower" needed. The effort came not in trying to stop but in simply taking the time to observe and journal their experience and spending more time paying attention to the present moment. Here are some of the mindfulness practices you can use to feel more empowered in the face of this affliction.

1. Breath-focused meditation

Set a timer for three minutes or longer and pay attention to your breathing. If your mind wanders, gently bring it back to your breath without judging or criticizing yourself. The key to mindful awareness is to accept whatever arises without criticism. You can find a guided breath-focused meditation online if you prefer to be talked through the practice. Take a moment now to breathe deeply and pay attention to your breath. Let your stomach fill with air when you inhale and count to at least four before you exhale loudly through your mouth. Paying attention to the way we breathe goes a long way toward soothing ourselves and preventing runaway thoughts.

2. Open-awareness meditation

Meditation does not mean wiping your mind clean of thoughts and making it into a blank slate. It can be as simple as setting a timer and letting your thoughts roam freely without judging them. If tears come when you sit and let your thoughts roam, these are emotions you've repressed while running around doing life at a hectic pace; what a blessing to give them space to breathe. You don't need to critique the emotions that come up or do anything about them right now. Let them be and allow them to flow through you.

3. Mindful body scan

This is a focused-attention meditation based on the body instead of the breath. A body scan is a mindfulness exercise in which you relax and bring focus to your physical body. Start by bringing your attention to your head. Slowly, make your way down your body paying attention to each part without judgment. Notice how each body part feels but don't try to change it. Is there any tension or pain? The body scan exercise does not ask you to relax or feel any different about your body, but simply focus on it. You can find many guided body scans on YouTube from a few minutes to a half hour in length.

I recommend searching online for a body scan of twenty minutes or more and following the guided instructions. You will be prompted to pay mindful attention to each part of your body separately, starting from your feet to your head or the reverse. Again, the idea is to notice your body without criticism or judgment. You may experience pain or tension, which you are encouraged to accept without wishing it were different. This is why mindfulness meditation is known to be effective in treating pain. Accepting the discomfort rather than resisting it can ease the unpleasantness of the sensation, proving again that what you resist persists. Some say the practice helps them connect with their bodies and notice where they hold stress and anxiety so they can release it. It also helps discipline a scattered mind by bringing thoughts into focus on a specific object (your body) in the present moment.

4. Mindful eating

One component of the MBSR program consists of a raisin-eating exercise. You literally eat a raisin mindfully, taking in the sight, smell, texture, and taste before, during, and after ingesting it. It doesn't have to be a raisin; any food will do. The practice can be used during any type of eating or drinking to slow down and pay attention to your body and what you're putting in it. Mindful eating can become a lifestyle in which you put aside distractions such as television or devices and focus on consuming your food. Since starting the practice, I've begun chewing my food twenty-five to thirty times before swallowing, which aids digestion and leaves me feeling more satisfied and less likely to eat more than I need.

I've also needed less variety in my food because the act of eating has become nourishing enough. Becoming more aware of my eating has helped me make healthier choices and mealtimes have become an act of self-care and self-nourishment. Food is more than fuel for our bodies; it's an experience for the senses. We want to slow down for mealtimes rather than rushing through eating on the way to the next thing.

5. Journal your triggers

Paying attention to what occurs immediately prior to a daydreaming session can help you feel more in control. Often, maladaptive daydreamers find themselves in the middle of a scenario and wonder how they got there. Writing down the trigger, which is often music, can help you become more mindful and even stay away from the source of activation, if desired. For example, you might delete songs from a playlist that you've identified in your journal as triggers. Sure, it's difficult to let go of music that brings you pleasure, but similar to drinking for some, you are deleting something from your life that many people can enjoy but that for you produces harmful effects.

6. Take a daily record of how long you daydream

Many maladaptive daydreamers spend the majority of their waking hours detached from reality and inside their mental playgrounds. Some will begin the moment they wake up and rarely stop until they go to sleep at night. They may even stay up late to continue daydreaming thereby losing sleep in addition to all the hours of the day lost to their habit. During the program, participants saw their daydreaming hours reduce dramatically. However, when you stop practicing mindfulness, you stop receiving its positive effects.

The mindfulness practices described in this lesson have benefits lasting long after the meditation sessions themselves are over. After a few weeks, you may notice that meditation has rewired your brain, making it less scattered and more functional, and that your escape fantasies have decreased significantly in both intensity and frequency. For the next week, implement a daily practice using at least one of the mindfulness practices previously discussed. A meditation session can last any length you desire, and many people start their day with one. Instead of reaching for a daydream, you can commit to a mindfulness practice, and chances are you will daydream less throughout the day. You can download a meditation app, find guided meditations online, or set a timer and sit while your thoughts and emotions roam freely without judgment or shame.

CHAPTER TWELVE

PARENTING YOURSELF

> "Many of us come out of childhood believing
> that what we have to say is as uninteresting
> to others as it was to our parents."
>
> PETE WALKER

PATRICIA CAME TO ME for help dealing with the aftermath of being raised by a narcissistic mother. As a child, she had been responsible for taking care of her mother's and siblings' needs, including cooking dinner and getting them ready for school, instead of receiving the care she needed as a young girl. Her mother used Patricia as a sounding board for her own emotions and threatened suicide regularly, blaming Patricia for her depressive thoughts. She recalled sitting in her classroom and feeling overwhelmed with anxiety over the fact that her mother might die, and it would be all her fault. As a result, she found it difficult to concentrate on her studies but excelled at visual art. She sought solace in drawing and painting, and continued these activities into adulthood, calling them her only source of pleasure.

In eighth grade, a teacher encouraged Patricia to apply for one of the coveted spots in the local high school's art program. The teacher offered to help her put together a portfolio and promised to write a glowing letter of recommendation. In spite of her instructor's efforts to help Patricia move in the direction of her obvious talent, Patricia declined the opportunity and attended the regular high school program that required no special application or effort. At the time, she experienced no regret over her decision and felt only relief over having avoided a potential threat. Unlike other students, she viewed a challenge such as applying for an art program as an opportunity to fail and look stupid rather than as a chance to grow and learn and stretch herself.

Described in Chapter 1, this phenomenon is a symptom of *survival brain,* common among survivors of childhood trauma. Rather than thinking long term, we decide how to protect ourselves from harm in the short term because that is what we've been tasked with our whole lives. If your parents were unreliable, abusive, neglectful, or worse, you fail to learn some basic life skills. Things like rising to challenges, healthy habits and routines, emotional regulation, and calculated risk-taking will feel foreign to you. You will not have learned the importance of doing things that scare you or pushing yourself beyond your comfort zone. In fact, you have no comfort zone because you live in a perpetual state of nervous system dysregulation brought on by the people who were supposed to love and protect you.

In some cases, your parents made you cater to their needs rather than taking care of yours, a situation called *parentification*. When parents fail to give children what they need, the child grows up feeling unheard and unseen, like they don't matter. In some cases, they will depersonalize or feel unreal, lacking a concrete sense of self upon which to build a life. Because our parents were crucial to our survival, inadequate parenting can leave the child feeling like the world is a scary place, no one is on her side, and she had only herself to lean on. All her energy and resources go into survival, which explains why Patricia would decline an opportunity that had the potential to change the trajectory of her life.

Unfortunately, this form of self-sabotage continues into adulthood and holds you back from real advancement and material opportunity. It contributes to your procrastination, which can be a form of self-protection from the outcome of completing a project. It's probable your work won't attain perfection and will draw attention to you. Both these outcomes may have gotten you rejected and abandoned as a child, so you avoid them through self-sabotage. Then you beat yourself up for your supposed laziness or cowardice, which only perpetuates the cycle of self-abuse.

You've grown up with a feeling of lack and deprivation, as if you don't deserve love or things other people enjoy. This becomes home for you and it's a programming that can feel impossible to overcome when you remain unaware of the root cause. You may hear a voice inside you that says, *That's not for you.* You only receive what others are willing to give to you and that has a devastating impact on your relationships and quality of life. You settle for less and sabotage connections with good people, for example, due to feeling unworthy of them and uncomfortable with anyone who treats you well.

Poor parenting in childhood negatively impacts our relationships, creates self-loathing and an intense inner critic, and leaves
us feeling unsupported and isolated. Those of us who suffered this
way are more likely to turn to substance abuse and experience
depression and suicidal thoughts. For example, I started drinking
as a teen to cope with my parents' severe emotional neglect. It was
the only time I felt comfortable in my skin and had the confidence
to speak my mind. When I drank, however, I'd get triggered by
something innocuous and fly into a rage. Regret over things I'd said
the night before became a regular occurrence. Now I know that
was the hurt child in me begging to be seen and heard and going
about it the wrong way. That unhealthy coping mechanism held me
back in every area of life and I had to learn to parent myself (and
give up alcohol) to live fully.

Parenting yourself means letting the hurt child feel heard and
seen. Otherwise, she'll try to get that attention in unhealthy ways
that feel beyond her control and that sabotage her. You parent yourself so you can receive the care and attention you lacked as a child
and live a more satisfying, authentic life. Until you learn to parent yourself, you'll keep seeking surrogate parents in toxic places.
This is why you end up with friends or romantic partners that hurt
you, or why you feel inferior to peers and coworkers. Without re-
parenting yourself, you'll keep repeating the same patterns that
hold you back and fail to establish routines necessary for success.
You'll continue giving up in the face of challenges because you
haven't learned the skill of long-term goal orientation. You'll keep
underachieving despite your immense potential, or overachieving
for the sole purpose of winning someone's love or validation. You'll
keep settling for less because that feels familiar to you.

When you start to care for yourself, however, your tolerance for pain and abuse will lower. You'll no longer feel comfortable in relationships where your needs are not met. You won't feel so desperate to hold on to someone who treats you like you don't matter. When you re-parent yourself, you begin to live a life that aligns with your values and makes you feel more like yourself. You discover who that "self" really is. Here are a few ways to begin the process of re-parenting yourself:

Self-kindness

Remember the first pillar of self-compassion and be kind to yourself. If you've been abused or neglected as a child, or had parents who weren't "good enough," you probably beat yourself up a lot. It's not realistic to say "Speak nicely to yourself." Behavior modification can be short-lived at best and useless at worst in the absence of a true shift in your beliefs about yourself. First, you must begin to treat yourself in ways that demonstrate you are valuable. When I got out of my toxic marriage and began my healing journey, I would not even allow myself the luxury of writing in my journal. I'd begin writing and my inner voice would stop me because I felt unworthy of spending time on myself. So, I understand if something as simple as journaling your thoughts and feelings seems difficult at first.

Start with something like sitting and doing nothing for five minutes. My daughter made me a door hanger at school for Mother's Day that read, "I need my mom time!" and I'd use it to sit alone in my room and decompress. It felt strange and wildly self-indulgent to sit by myself for ten or fifteen minutes, but that was the beginning of me parenting myself, even though I didn't call it that at the time. The more I did it the more familiar it became, and I created a new normal for myself that placed a chip in my brain that said, *You're worth it.* Those moments in my room marked the beginning of my mindfulness journey, though I was not aware of it at the time.

Start saying no to things that don't interest you and yes to things that scare you but excite you. Taking time to understand your likes and dislikes and doing more of what pleases you will help you value yourself more. Find a hobby or passion and do it because you love it, not as a job.

Pay attention to what you do well and ask trusted friends and loved ones to help you with your list. If your parents never helped you know your strengths and weaknesses, this is the time to find them out for yourself. You may be getting to know yourself for the first time. All your life you've been surviving and defending yourself against external threats rather than looking within. Kindly exploring yourself this way will help change your inner voice from one of criticism and loathing to loving and cherishing.

Self-discipline

As a child, you missed not only nurturing, but structure and discipline because of under-parenting. In fact, loving parents can over-nurture and fail to discipline their children, although I'd argue that's not loving at all. So, in addition to learning self-care and nurturing, you need to discipline yourself as well. Just as the best parents offer a balance of soothing and structure, you need to teach yourself the necessary life skills of establishing routines, delaying gratification, and sticking with challenges even when everything in you wants to give up. If your parents never taught you the value of such structures, it's natural you'll struggle to develop them. This leaves you at a huge disadvantage in getting what you want out of life since most things worth having come from sticking to a plan, repeating tasks, and taking good care of yourself. As mentioned in Chapter 1, making lunch every day before work keeps you healthy and financially fit. Going to bed and waking up at the same time makes you more alert and refreshed.

Reaching goals requires doing the same things over and over. If you've never learned these basic life skills, you may not realize how important they are. In the same way challenges are difficult for the traumatized brain, sticking with mundane routines feels excruciating for someone who never received good parenting. Remember, the traumatized brain wants to get things over with rather than explore with playful curiosity. That's why sticking with the tasks that lead to success is more difficult when you have no guarantee of the outcome. You fear failure more than other people do because you were not allowed to test and try things as a youngster. That fear subconsciously stops you from moving forward because if you give up, at least you didn't fail. So, parenting yourself is not only about obvious forms of self-care but also self-discipline and establishing healthy routines. It's loving yourself enough to follow through on the promises you make to yourself.

Find joy

When self-help experts tell you to remember how you felt in childhood to reclaim your joy, do you feel alone or embarrassed or maybe roll your eyes? It is entirely possible to recollect not one joyful moment from childhood and therefore have no point of reference for the feeling. The rare moments of joy I remember were invariably followed by an adult chastising me for having fun. Once, when I stayed after school to play with my classmates, my mother lambasted me for my lateness. What sounds like an innocuous incident contributed to my hypervigilance and inability to let go and enjoy myself. A switch flipped in me that day equating fun with punishment and the familiar fear of abandonment by my primary caregiver.

While it's natural to express worry over a child's whereabouts, my mother made it all about her and refused to acknowledge me at all. Besides, she had never told me to come home right after school, so I faced punishment despite breaking no rules, a common theme in my home. This is how dysfunctional parents move the goalposts. They establish no rules or routines but punish you for actions you had no way of knowing were forbidden. That fear of reprimand without cause or based on unpredictable triggers like your parent's feelings at the time, stays with you throughout adulthood. When someone asks to speak with you, or every time the phone rings, does a chill go down your spine? You assume you're going to get in trouble, even though you've done nothing wrong.

Despite my difficult childhood, I remember finding solace in solitary activities like Barbies, rug hooking, coloring, and paper dolls. These healthy self-soothing endeavors gave me peace in a chaotic environment. Though I wouldn't describe them as joy-filled, they were close enough that I revisited solitary activities as an adult learning to parent myself. Exploring childhood activities that brought you pleasure will remind you it's okay to do things for fun and personal fulfillment, without having a monetary purpose or responsibility for someone else.

Express emotions

When we suppress our emotions, unhealthy self-soothing can result. We sabotage ourselves through substance abuse, compulsive shopping, and overeating. These coping mechanisms distract us from the feelings we stuff down and help us cope with the disconnect we experience while living inauthentic lives. If our parents ignored our feelings or punished us for them, it's logical we would stop expressing them, even to ourselves.

You can train your mind to lie to you through the power of positive thinking. But this refusal to face reality results in adverse effects, such as chronic illness in middle age. Dr. Gabor Maté gives ample evidence that suppressing anger results in all kinds of illnesses. He believes it accounts for the higher numbers of women who suffer with chronic diseases since women have been conditioned to abandon themselves and cater to others while suppressing their resentment. He says if you let your emotional needs go unmet and unspoken for a lifetime, your body finally says, "Enough!" So, how can you acknowledge your emotions and avoid health risks that come with suppressing unpleasant feelings?

Set aside regular time to write down your thoughts and feelings. This helps you process your emotions and bring them out in the open. Beginning to write simply to connect with yourself can mark the start of a healing journey. You may have no idea how much goes on inside of you until you begin to get it out on paper. Even if you're not a fan of journaling, schedule regular time alone to process your emotions. Busyness can mask your true feelings and distract you from creating needed change in your life. You consume yourself with the minutiae of the day-to-day, cater to everyone else's needs, and neglect your own as an avoidance strategy.

Suppressed emotions come to the surface quickly when you stop the constant doing. Try not to fight feelings when they appear but observe and let them give you information. This is the mindful self-compassion we've discussed in the previous chapter. For instance, anger can tell you what needs to change in your life, and you can take baby steps to make that happen. Search for "films that make you cry" if you need help bringing your sadness to the surface. I often have blocked tears due to a lifetime of emotional suppression, and I remember watching the animated film *Inside Out* to help me release them. Sometimes, sharing in someone else's pain, even a character, can help you get in touch with your own. A good cry can be cathartic, and a tearjerker will help you get those feelings into the open where they belong.

Grieve Your Lost Childhood

Grief here means celebrating something good that's now missing from your life. By this definition, grieving a lost childhood means honoring the innocence taken from you when innocence was equated with danger and hurt. It means drawing out that playfulness and curiosity you never experienced as a child. Children in healthy households learn by trial and error, and feel free to explore thanks to their secure attachment figures. You have the opportunity to practice that playfulness now.

Grieving your lost childhood means letting down your hypervigilance and need to control, and letting things unfold. If you get hurt, it's not the end of the world. You have the inner stores as an adult to acknowledge and praise your courage to get outside your comfort zone. You have learned the self-compassion strategies to help you look within for your strength rather than seeking validation outside of you. Grieving means acknowledging your needs weren't met, and this led you to believe those needs aren't important. But your needs do matter, and you are not selfish to want to have them fulfilled. So, how can you begin to take care of those needs today?

The first step is figuring out what those needs are if you've suppressed them. For example, I began to take care of my deep desire for time alone to reflect. I had denied this need all my life and filled my days with self-sacrificial tasks and activities that only made me feel more detached from my true self. If I found myself with free time, I'd feel too guilty to read a book and would instead fill that time with obligations like cleaning the house. I didn't value myself enough to spend my time doing something that felt good to me.

Now I spend most of my time doing things that feel good or align with my values and the goals I've set for myself. I have little trouble saying no and feel free to explore new relationships and get out of them if they're not meeting my needs. I believe the same can be true for you if you implement the practices you've learned in this book throughout your daily life. Spending time with yourself and paying attention to your thoughts and emotions will help you connect more deeply with yourself.

Setting boundaries around your time and gravitating toward things you've determined you value will bring a lasting change in your quality of life. Replacing the harsh self-talk with mindful self-compassion will add a dimension of self-awareness that just reciting positive mantras lacks. You may have learned the opposite as a child, but you are the most important person in your life, and you matter. It may seem counterintuitive, but you serve the world and the people around you by caring for your own needs well. In the words of Howard Thurman, the American author and civil rights leader: "Don't ask what the world needs. Ask what makes you come alive and go do it. Because what the world needs is more people who have come alive."

CHAPTER THIRTEEN

FORGIVING YOURSELF AND OTHERS

"Forgiveness is giving up the hope
that the past could be any different."
OPRAH WINFREY

YOU'VE HEARD THE WARNING about refusing to forgive, that it is like drinking poison and expecting the other person to die. If you come from a faith background, you may have learned that forgiveness is holy and required by God. If you don't forgive others, God won't forgive you. To others it means letting people off the hook when they've harmed you, even when they offer no apology or amends. As a result of cultural conditioning, you might take for granted that forgiveness is necessary for healing.

All this can make forgiveness feel like an obligation you must accept to move forward in your healing journey. It's as if forgiveness is the magic ticket to a life of freedom from resentment and ill will. For that reason, you might feel tempted to fast-track your forgiveness to obtain those good feelings. Or you may think you have no choice but to forgive someone who's hurt you. After all, we're bombarded with images and videos of people forgiving criminals of murder and other heinous acts, so who are we to deny the same courtesy to someone whose transgressions appear far less egregious?

It's important to ask yourself if you think you can't move on without forgiving because society has trained you to believe that. When you feign forgiveness before you're prepared to give it, you harm yourself through self-abandonment and inauthenticity—the very systems of self-sabotage you're learning to release throughout this book. Only you can decide if you're ready to forgive and, if you're not, that position deserves respect and support. Forgiveness should never feel forced, nor should the motive come from external sources. When forgiveness comes from a place of obligation and cultural conditioning, there's a danger of people-pleasing, which is exactly what you're trying to avoid.

Many advise a "fake it till you make it" approach when it comes to forgiving others. They say you should do so *before* you feel like it because the feelings may never come. Forgiveness is seen as so necessary that you must override your true feelings to grant it. Once again, this approach flies in the face of everything you've learned in this book, primarily the pillar of self-compassion that says accepting and acknowledging your feelings is a key to self-healing. You've also learned the views and research of trauma-informed medical expert Gabor Maté, who says unexpressed anger manifests as dis-ease. That means overriding your true feelings to offer forgiveness to another can literally make you sick.

The adage about taking poison and expecting the other person to die supports the societal view that anger and resentment should go unacknowledged. Feelings are not something we can simply let go of at will, however. When forgiveness is given before processing the anger, the victim or survivor is forced to suppress their own needs. Compelling yourself to forgive before you're ready means denying your true feelings, and that's exactly what you're learning to stop doing. It's another form of self-abandonment designed to make others feel better. What if you focused instead on the won-derful information you receive from your anger, instead of once again feeling responsible for repairing what someone else broke?

Remember from Chapter 3 that family scapegoats often bear the burden of responsibility for repairing and maintaining relation-ships. You may be falling into old patterns of trying to prove your goodness by "taking the high road," which will only enable your abuser and prevent forward movement in your life. Our society has a funny way of encouraging the victim to do the hard work of reconciliation while the abuser receives protection. Survivors often feel guilty for a lack of forgiveness—even if no one's asked for it or apologized. That might be okay if forgiveness always promoted healing and helped a survivor move on, but it sometimes creates cognitive dissonance instead. It keeps the survivor in a pattern of denying her true feelings and telling herself something she doesn't believe.

Oprah Winfrey says forgiveness means "giving up the hope that the past could be any different." As an operating definition of forgiveness, this one works for the purposes of this chapter. There's power in *accepting* that you cannot change the past or control the future. In my experience with clients, most of their suffering comes from the wish that things could have been different and their family members (or whoever caused them harm) will change. The constant need to know why they did what they did only keeps you stuck and frustrated. Believing you need them to change and understand you before you can move on will prevent you from doing so. The mindfulness exercises we've discussed in previous chapters will help you maintain present-moment awareness instead of dwelling on the past or projecting into the future. It will instill in you the new core belief that the past is over and the future unwritten; peace and happiness lie in embracing the here and now.

I find it interesting that every time I post a caption on Instagram about dysfunctional family dynamics, at least a few people chastise me for being too hard on my parents. What they fail to realize is that I've taken the focus off my parents and put it on myself and my own healing. My interest lies in the impact of my caregivers' actions on me, not the actions themselves or who made them. It really has nothing to do with them. If your first inclination when addressing the effect of abuse or unmet needs on your life is to protect your parents, I urge you to break that pattern. True healing requires an honest and cohesive narrative of what happened to you, not excuses and justifications for bad behavior.

Instead of letting people off the hook, forgiveness can mean accepting their limitations. You can stay away from someone and still forgive them. That means you maintain a critical distance or even the no-contact rule we discussed in Chapter 5 while benefiting from the choice to accept that you cannot rewrite the past.

Forgiveness and trust are two separate things, and it would be fool-ish to allow someone back into your life who's proven they will only harm you. By our working definition, forgiveness has nothing to do with reconciliation. You can forgive someone without seeing them again or them ever knowing.

If you've dealt with a narcissist or toxic person, you've prob-ably already gone through a cycle of allowing someone back into your life only for them to disappoint you again. I went through this pattern with my mother for decades. She would write me off for saying no to one of her requests, and then resume communication as if nothing had happened. I finally realized I was not obligated to allow my mother back into my life only to hurt me over and over. Her refusal to see me as a separate human being with my own needs and desires became intolerable as I began to demand more as a result of my personal growth journey.

Rather than focus on forgiving my mother, I decided to turn that energy toward myself and my own healing. I spent time pro-cessing my resentment toward her through angry letters (that went unsent, of course) and journaling entries that outlined her transgressions against me. I stopped making excuses for her or feeling guilty about our estrangement. In fact, it was she who ini-tiated estrangement over and over throughout the decades as she detached from me for daring to set the smallest boundary with her. I began to see the dynamic between us more clearly as I stopped scrambling to pick up pieces she had thrown on the ground.

During a recent podcast interview, the host asked if I'd for-given my mother, and I felt surprised to realize that I had. This forgiveness had come from processing my righteous anger and resentment, telling the truth about the situation, and turning the gaze on myself rather than on my mother. When I stopped expecting her to behave any differently and gave up the fantasy that she would change, I gained freedom. Of course, change is possible for anyone, and I can't predict the future, but I have no control over her actions. The realization that I felt no emotional charge when I thought about my mother gave me proof that I had forgiven her. Rather than a conscious choice, this release came about organically from doing the work on myself to recover from the toxic family dynamics I'd navigated all my life.

Authentic forgiveness comes when you stop pressuring yourself into it and focus on your own healing instead. After you process your rightful anger and resentment, you may find yourself thinking less and less about your abuser. As your life improves and the person loses control over you, your resentment decreases but anger might remain—and that's okay. Anger has its place as a guardian of your heart and reminds you of what you endured and why you should never go back. Forced forgiveness comes from the same mindset that views anger in a negative light. Let's normalize seeing anger as your friend.

I've come to believe forgiving yourself is more important than forgiving others. Often, we blame ourselves for what happened as though we should have done something to stop it. This is an area where we can let go of the hope that our past could have been different. When we've experienced pain or abuse at the hands of others and we have yet to process that, we might turn around and inflict pain on others. When we've vowed never to be like our parents, we are shocked to hear their words flying out of our mouths. It can seem like the harder you try not to do something, the more likely it is to happen. I've heard people say their philosophy of child-rearing is to do the opposite of their parents, but overidentification with your past wounds is no way to navigate through life. Although well-intentioned, it keeps the focus on your parents' actions, and you remain beholden to them even as you try to be nothing like them.

What you focus on expands, so using your caregivers as a negative compass will likely result in you emulating them against your better judgment. This causes a disempowering sense of shame when you realize you have less control over your behavior than you thought. Setting yourself up as the antidote to your parents' bullying or neglect will not effect the kind of change that transforms generational trauma. Creating your own unique brand of parenting that comes from a place of healing rather than a wound will create that change and it won't feel like white-knuckling or trying to be perfect. When you make vows to be nothing like your parents, the shame that comes with making mistakes that impact others, especially loved ones, only causes you to act out again. That's because shame never works, but self-compassion does.

As a parent with complex PTSD, you are likely harder on yourself than other parents. This is in part because you were conditioned in childhood to believe you had to be perfect to be okay. You are also harder on yourself in general because this is how you coped with the abuse or neglect in your childhood. It gave you a sense of control to believe that striving for perfection would win you love and acceptance. If you forgive yourself for your imperfections, recognize every parent gets it wrong sometimes, and stop overidentifying with your transgressions, you will be less likely to repeat them. Remember Dr. Winnicott's advice from Chapter 3: it's how you treat your children overall that matters, not whether you get it right every time. It's natural to dwell on your mistakes more than your victories, but good parents need not be perfect, only consistent. Winnicott said that not only are mistakes in parenting inevitable, but your children benefit when you fail from time to time. Making mistakes as a parent provides an opportunity to make amends and show your children you're human. This gives them a model for how to repair things when a relationship breaks down. It's a chance to show them the love and respect they deserve.

Benefits of Authentic Forgiveness

Remember, if you choose to forgive, it's for yourself and not the other person. You're letting yourself, rather than them, off the hook and they may not even know (or care) that you've forgiven them. You've probably heard that you should consider what happened to your abuser to make them behave the way they do. However, this has nothing to do with how their behavior affected you and should not become the focus of your energy. Forgiveness does not erase what the person did to you or the consequences of their actions on your life. You still need to process your emotions, especially anger, and grieve over what happened to you. Grieving does not need to be complete for you to forgive if you choose to, but it is necessary so you can move forward authentically, without stuffing down unprocessed emotions.

Here are four benefits you'll gain from forgiving those who hurt you (that have nothing to do with *them*). By forgive we mean letting go of the hope that the past could be any different. It means releasing them from the need to change and accepting their limitations whether you decide to have an ongoing relationship with them or not.

1. Stress reduction

Negative feelings normally accompany unforgiveness. When you want things in the past to be different than they were, that creates a lot of stress and tension in the body. Stress releases chemicals that can cause physical illness and the constant tension holds you back from living your best life. When you release someone through forgiveness you choose to release yourself from undue stress. This has the power to improve your health and help you move forward toward the life of your dreams. Understanding how releasing someone through authentic forgiveness lowers anxiety, stress, and blood pressure helps you see its value. It boosts your immune system and increases self-esteem while improving relationships, both present and future.

2. Forgiveness and trust are distinct

Forgiving someone does not mean you have to trust them. If your spouse had an affair, for example, and makes sincere efforts to change, you can forgive before trust has been reestablished. It's ludicrous to suggest that you should magically trust someone because they've apologized and expressed remorse for a wrongdoing. Reestablishing trust takes time and work on the part of the perpetrator whose responsibility it is to earn back your trust. If someone grows impatient with your need for time to win back trust after they've betrayed you, that's a red flag.

When you forgive, you still take measures to protect yourself. For example, you can forgive someone while removing them from your life because they've shown an unwillingness to change. Saying sorry is not enough if the person who hurt you keeps repeating the same patterns over and over. Your decision to keep taking them back despite their reluctance to change enables them to keep doing what they're doing. This was the dynamic between my mother and me (and she never apologized, which shows you how conditioned I'd been to take responsibility for her bad behavior). You may fear putting yourself in harm's way if you extend forgiveness to someone who keeps hurting you, but that only happens if you allow the abuse to go on. You can forgive someone and refuse to reconcile with them; that's healthy self-protection. Forgiving someone with whom you've gone no contact, for example, still offers you health benefits.

3. When you forgive you release resentment

I'm willing to bet that, like my clients, much of your unhappiness has come from wishing things were different, either now or in the past (or both). So much of my pain came from the fantasy that one day other people would change and understand me. I remained unhappy because I'd put my focus on matters and people outside of my control, mainly my unsupportive family and the things they'd done to me. Both—the past and other people—are wholly outside my control. However, I couldn't let go of their hold on me until I learned the art of staying present.

People had been telling me to let things go my whole adult life (and you've probably heard the same advice). Not until I began a mindfulness practice could I begin to enjoy the present without dwelling too much on the past. A simple breathwork or meditation session could leave me euphoric, a feeling I'd only believed possible with something outside myself, like drugs or sex. It's empowering to realize you need little more than attention to your breath to experience pure happiness. All the effort I'd put into the false

belief other people needed to change for me to be happy fell away.
When I learned to turn my gaze within instead of outward toward
family members (who had shown me how much they disliked and
disrespected me), *everything changed.*

---

4. When you forgive, it alters your identity

Refusing or resisting forgiveness can become your unwanted identity. You label yourself the victim of your perpetrator, which makes
it difficult to move on. Your mind may be consumed with thoughts
of revenge or fantasies that the person will finally understand you.
You experience intense frustration over their behavior toward you
even though it's been going on for years. I'm not advocating forgive and forget, and I strongly believe in grieving past events for as
long as you need to. But extending forgiveness can help you forge a
new identity. When you forgive, you become the hero of your own
story, one who's no longer limited by the wrongs done against you
in the past. You're free to chart a course independent of another's
influence or crimes against you.

Joseph Campbell has written about the hero's journey, one
in which you are called to an adventure you cannot refuse (even
though you try at first). You then go through a series of challenges
and trials that must be overcome to achieve your transformation.
At the end, you return renewed and finally able to live freely and
authentically. You've courageously faced your fears and refused to
hide from the truth, which puts you in an elite class. You've gone
above and beyond in the pursuit of happiness and that has enhanced
your sense of self-worth. You've set boundaries that dictate what
you will and won't tolerate and you've refused to repeat old patterns that let others misuse or mistreat you. You may notice that

your enhanced self-image attracts advice seekers on how they can get what you have. Now, you can teach them what you've learned and help them improve their lives and break generational cycles. If you have children, this is the greatest gift you will ever give them.

CHAPTER FOURTEEN

CLEANING OUT YOUR CLOSET

"Have nothing in your houses
that you do not know to be useful
or believe to be beautiful."

WILLIAM MORRIS

I DISCOVERED THE BENEFITS of decluttering when I
moved from a house to a condo many years ago. The upkeep of a
two-story dwelling had taken its toll on this divorced mom both
physically and financially. Truth be told, I'd always wanted to live
in a condo and my divorce helped me start paying the tiniest bit of
attention to what I wanted and move toward that. Only problem?
We would have to downsize our possessions to fit into the new
space. That presented no problem logistically as I'm an efficient

and organized person by nature. Streamlining is my middle name. However, my struggle came from the social conditioning that had me believe downsizing represented a step backward. Success means growth, not shrinking, but I had yet to learn the most important growth happens on the inside.

The more we purged, the easier it became to say goodbye to things that had outlived their usefulness. I had believed downsizing was the price to pay for the lifestyle that suited me. The truth that decluttering only improved our lives and offered no downside came as a surprise. Deciding what to keep and give away helped me get clear on what mattered to me most. If I didn't find it useful or beautiful, as William Morris quipped, it had to go. Curating my life this way helped me set boundaries in other areas of my life and feel more in control of my destiny. Owning fewer things created literal space to figure out who I was and what I wanted. Clearing out physical clutter in my environment made it easier to tackle the mental and emotional baggage stored inside me. Something about removing years of useless trash imbued me with courage to pare down in other areas of my life as well.

You might not think about values, boundaries, or self-sabotage when you consider decluttering, but there is a psychological component to the practice that cannot be denied. Although decluttering seems like a physical activity, it has a mental and even spiritual effect on you because your surroundings reflect what's going on inside of you. The horror you feel when you see the homes of hoarders immediately translates into sympathy or curiosity over what's going on inside of the people who hoard. You have a felt sense that healthy people do not stockpile possessions this way. By the same token, you may admire minimalists for their self-discipline, discretion, and even care for the planet.

How you treat your space reflects the way you treat yourself. You may avoid addressing fundamental problems in your life and relationships and that plays out in you avoiding certain drawers, rooms, or spaces in your home. We hold on to things that no longer serve us (and probably never did) because we refuse to look at them and do the work of sorting the treasure from the trash. Decluttering helps you examine and take inventory of your possessions and determine which ones still have a place in your life. It's no coincidence that step four in the twelve-step program involves taking a searching and fearless moral inventory of your life. Here are four of the many benefits you'll experience when you declutter your home and environment:

1. Reduced stress

In the documentary *A Cluttered Life: Middle-Class Abundance,* a team of anthropologists went into the homes of thirty-two, dual-income American families. They discovered these families had accumulated so much stuff it put a marked strain on their mental health. An overabundance of food, toys, and clothing created stress in the mothers, especially. Men didn't remark on the clutter or seem to notice it as much because they were not the ones responsible for cleaning it up. Although unspoken, women felt responsible for organizing and tidying even though they worked outside the home, too. There is evidence that women find it harder to compartmentalize, so clutter will impact them more significantly since they can't shut it out.

For most people, it's hard to relax in a cluttered room. Trying to decompress after a hard day in a space strewn with stuff is all but impossible. You spend your downtime reorganizing junk or putting things away rather than putting your feet up. That builds frustration, the opposite of what you want when your goal is to unwind. Every day, you experience the tension of time spent looking for items. Kids are late for school because they can't find their shoes or books. Pressure trickles down to your loved ones who bear the brunt of your annoyance, not to mention the effect on your own peace of mind. Clutter in your surroundings hurts your ability to focus. The extraneous items in your field of vision take you away from the task at hand. Whether you have to physically clear the items, or simply take note of them in your mind, clutter divides your attention, which can negatively impact your productivity. Clearing the clutter in your home alleviates all these stressors.

2. Better boundaries

My college friend had an excessive collection of ceramic pigs scattered around her house, so I assumed she had a penchant for the cute pink mammals. Turns out she got a pig once as a gift and they just kept coming. She's completely indifferent to the animals but never had the nerve to tell people to stop giving them to her. Her clutter reflected an unwillingness to set boundaries as she put *their* desire to give ahead of her own need to have dominion over what takes up space in her home.

Going clutter-free stops this type of self-sabotage by helping you set limits. You've started by setting boundaries with yourself when you decided what to keep or toss. You overcame your avoidance and fears of what people might think to create an environment that's meaningful to you. Courage begets courage and you'll draw on those stores to set boundaries with others when it comes to your own space. Unlike my friend with the pigs, you'll start to confront people gently when they keep giving you things you don't want. You've learned the magic word no and will use it until you get comfortable saying it. As a result, your thinking shifts so you're no longer prioritizing others' feelings over your values and chosen lifestyle.

As we learned in Chapter 4, you knew deep down some people wouldn't like your boundaries, so you avoided the confrontation. That kept you small and took a toll on your soul you may not have realized. Now you know the ones who disrespect your new boundaries are the most important reason you need to set them. You have to teach people how to treat you. Truth is, you have the power to say no to things before those things ever cross the threshold of your front door, and that may involve a dreaded "difficult conversation." For instance, you'll set limits on the number of presents your kids receive from family and you will meet resistance. If you're like me and hate conflict, that will be hard, but reducing clutter means confronting what's not working in your life. Hopefully, you're beginning to see how you deal with deeper issues when you begin to get control of your living space. That means setting appropriate boundaries and putting your need for a clutter-free home ahead of others' desire to bring more into it.

3. Clarity on your values

Downsizing helps you hone and refine your values. When you're deciding what to keep and what to throw away, you determine what matters to you. Often, that stuff is tied to an image we have of ourselves as a successful person. You or your spouse traded a lot of time in the form of work hours to buy those things. However, letting go of external pressures when it comes to the size of your house or model of your car gives you license to pursue what's important to you. You move further from the world's definition of success and closer to your own. It's impossible to know what you value when your life has been determined by other peoples' opinions, whether real or imagined. Living with less creates space in your mind as well as your environment for what lights you up. More streamlined surroundings translate into better mental focus and that helps you drill down and realize your goals.

4. Improved confidence

Successful decluttering of your space feels like a major achievement because you've done something most people lack the fortitude to carry out. You're facing an issue head-on and refusing to settle for less than you deserve. You've made tough decisions about what stays or what goes. As you decide what to keep or donate, you get to know yourself better as you discover your likes and dislikes. When you look around and see a space you feel proud to call your own, your confidence increases, and you feel in control of your life. When you start living with less, it's a practice of removing physical clutter, but the more you get into it, the more philosophical it becomes.

How to Know if You Need to Declutter

Extensive decluttering advice is outside the scope of this book, but the following three questions will help you determine if you need to take this step. It's important to note we each have our own idea of comfort. For some people, knickknacks make a home cozy while for others they represent clutter. Extreme minimalism can signify unhealthy self-denial as much as hoarding relates to avoidance. In fact, I had to reconcile my refusal to buy myself nice things in the name of reducing clutter and saving the planet. Now I enjoy a healthy balance between a streamlined environment and those creature comforts that make me feel loved.

1. Does my living space reflect who I am?

When you look around do you think, *Yes, this makes me feel good and I'm proud to call this my space,* or are you like my friend whose home is scattered with ceramic pigs she never wanted? When sitting in your living area, do you look around and breathe easy? Do your things serve a purpose, or do you wonder why you bought them? One mind trick we play on ourselves is the "sunk cost" fallacy. You think since you paid for something, you're obligated to keep it but the mental cost of holding on to things that misalign with your values is greater than any financial one. You're not getting that money back whether the thing goes or stays, so why not get rid of it?

2. Am I being honest about what I want?

When you set boundaries with people around gift giving, you're helping them understand your expectations. Though they may not like it, you're demonstrating that you care more about them than what they give you. You care enough to be honest with them rather than harbor resentment. Instead of exchanging physical gifts, you might suggest spending time together. Sharing conversation over a meal provides a bonding experience no material thing can.

If someone digs in their heels and refuses to adapt, that gives you important information. Now you get to decide how much space this person will take up in your life. That's one way external decluttering leads to internal decluttering. In the same way you choose items for your home that give you pleasure, you may opt to spend less time with those who add little to your life. Reducing or eliminating time spent with difficult people will have a positive impact on your physical and mental health. For a refresher on how to deal with toxic people, reread Chapter 5.

3. Am I doing more of what I want or don't want?

Are you spending more time on activities you enjoy rather than on obligations? You know now that downsizing is about more than physical clutter and impacts all areas of your life, including how you fill your schedule and the people you spend time with. Maybe your calendar is filled with obligations that leave you feeling unfulfilled and you're spending too much time with people who drain you. Decluttering will spearhead your journey to stopping these self-sabotaging activities that hold you back from the life you desire. It sets the stage for adopting healthy boundaries, determining your values, making better decisions, and creating the life you want. Most of all, it makes the impossible attainable. Maybe you never genuinely believed you'd get out from underneath your clutter, so when you do, your brain says, *Okay, what's next?*

Next, look at the way you spend your time and declutter your calendar. Look at with whom you spend that time and prioritize certain relationships over others. Sadly, you may have to eliminate some altogether because there is no way for you to grow and expand into the person you were meant to be amid their negative influence. The courage to cut ties with toxic people mirrors the courage it takes to let go of things in your home that no longer serve you. When you successfully declutter your home, you begin to create a life to your specifications rather than one formed from reacting and surviving, and that impacts other areas.

As with any foray into self-growth and development, decluttering your home is best approached in baby steps. I suggest starting with one room or even a drawer. Your clothes closet serves as a good beginning point because it's small, manageable, and devoted to you. This way you won't confuse self-care with serving others as you might when you clear out a common area. Cleaning out your closet also serves as an apt metaphor for getting rid of all the stuff in your life that's holding you back.

To help ease overwhelm, I thought it would be fun to share the system I used to clean out my own closet. A stylist friend of mine walked me through this process over a decade ago and I've never had to do it again. All that's required now is to maintain the system once it's in place. This exercise will provide you with a physical representation of the work you're doing on yourself: a streamlined, organized, and edited closet that contains only items you love and that make you look and feel great. My guess is that a renewed wardrobe will inspire you to declutter other areas of your home as well. However, using the mindfulness lessons you've learned so far in this book, I encourage you to focus on the task in front of you with a spirit of presence and self-compassion. That means no beating yourself up over clothes that don't fit you or that you've never worn. Rather than rushing through to the end, treat this as a meditative practice where you are inside the present moment, neither looking ahead nor behind. You can create an intention for your practice that will help you stay focused.

Without further ado, I give you my version of the five-step system for a one-and-done closet declutter.

1. Try everything on

The first step is to try on everything you own. Make sure you set aside ample time for this task, which is the foundation for the other steps. It sounds tiresome but won't take as long as you think. As you try on each item, place them in one of four piles. See step two below.

2. Make four piles: keep, alter, donate, and toss

If something fits and looks good on you, keep it. If it needs alteration to fit you today, send it to the seamstress. Alterations are an investment, so decide if the item is worth it to you. (In case you've never used a seamstress, try your local dry cleaner, or there's one in most shopping malls.) If something neither fits, looks good, nor can be altered, place it in the donation pile. If it hasn't been worn in a year or more, it probably won't be, so donate that, too. There are exceptions to this rule, such as special occasion dresses, so use your judgment. You can make money selling rather than donating quality items online or on consignment, another bonus when you declutter your closet. If an item is too old, worn, or torn to be donated, place it in the toss pile.

This step is simple but not easy. It challenges you to let go of things you've been holding on to for a long time, and we're not only talking about clothes here. It requires you to accept yourself as you are *today*, not as you were before you had kids, or as you imagine you might be in three months. Here's a chance to implement the mindful self-compassion you learned about in Chapter 6. Rather than berate yourself if you've gained weight, love yourself by ridding your closet of clothes that no longer fit. You do not have to give up weight-loss goals but accepting yourself as you are now will go a longer way to fulfilling them in the future.

3. Organize the clothes that made the cut

After you've tried on all your clothes and determined which ones will stay, you may be amazed to see your closet reduced by half or more. Organize the remaining items in a way that pleases your eye. I like to sort by shade, from light to dark, but choose a system that works for you. Replace your wire and plastic hangers with good ones that match. The uniformity will inspire peace and pleasure when you look at your closet, and the quality is better for your clothes and makes you feel better about them. Your newly edited closet will replace chaos with calm, so you feel happy when you look at it (rather than stressed) and rewarded for all your hard work.

4. Practice one in/one out

The key to retaining a low-clutter closet is to keep no extra hangers. That way, when something new comes in, something old must go out. This will help you become more mindful about your clothes-buying practices, the same way you're careful about who you let into your life (to stretch the metaphor). You'll no longer indulge in shopping as a mindless activity or, heaven forbid, as therapy. If you buy something new to wear, you must decide what will go out to make room for the new item. This helps keep clutter from reappearing and has the added benefit of saving you tons of money.

5. Enjoy extra money and peace of mind

Now that you are the proud owner of an expertly decluttered closet, you'll feel calmer as you face fewer decisions in the morning about what to wear. Your self-image blossoms when everything you own fits well and flatters you. In addition, you'll see a difference in your bank balance when you stop buying clothes so often. What will you do with all that extra money now that you stopped shopping so often? Start a retirement fund? Plan a vacation? It sounds extravagant now but wait and see how much you save when you stop clothes shopping and enjoy what you already own. Think about the *Sex and the City* episode in which Carrie realizes with regret that she has spent $40,000 on shoes that could have gone toward a down payment for a home.

In the process of downsizing your possessions you may come up against some long-held beliefs that need to be challenged. Most of us have been socialized to equate success with financial abundance. We feel we must keep up with our neighbors, even when the little voice inside tells us that's not what we value. As a young mother, I constantly gauged what others did to tell me how I ought to live. Little did I know, most of them were doing the same thing! Living uncluttered means letting go of what people think at the same time as you release possessions. It means going against the grain and living counter to the culture and requires courage at times and sacrifice at others. You become driven by the desire to live according to what you believe in and to take control of your surroundings.

That's the dual purpose of decluttering: to help you reenvision your environment and discover more about yourself in the process. It helps you prioritize your own needs rather than putting yourself last. This is how downsizing your closet sets the stage for pruning in all areas of your life. You start decluttering one room and end up transforming your life. The same can be said for the stones you turn over and examine when you decide you can no longer tolerate an inauthentic life where your needs go unmet. Throughout this book we've gone on a journey to help you uncover the blind spots holding you back. As you've learned, most of those subconscious barriers to your success have their roots in past trauma.

I'm no houseplant expert—in fact, I've killed my fair share of the poor creatures. While researching how to nurture one of these back to life, I learned you have to pull up and cut off the dead roots and discard them so the rest of the plant can flourish. If left to fester, they will take over and kill the plant. These rotten roots can go undetected because they lie below the surface, unseen. However, their effect on the plant manifests itself in discolored leaves and stunted growth. In the same way, when you avoid dealing with the root of your pain, which is past trauma, it will prevent you from growing and flourishing as your highest self. You have to be willing to look beneath the surface to find those rotten roots—which can be painful—and cut them out so you can thrive.

After removal of the dead roots, the plant finds a new home in fresh soil where it has a chance to survive. The organism cannot thrive in the same environment that made its roots rot and die. Usually that's a container with too much water and poor drainage. For you, the environment may be a home or a relationship or an extended family contributing to your demise. Before you take any drastic action like moving to a new city or filing for divorce, turn the gaze toward yourself. The Buddhist monk Thich Nhat Hanh famously wrote, "The way out is in." By looking underneath the surface and tending to your own root system, you'll begin to flourish in ways that are impossible when you're gazing outward. Whether that's in outrage over behavior that's remained unchanged for decades, or the erroneous belief that you need them to understand you before you can feel peace, giving others control over your destiny will only ensure that you never fulfill it.

It's painful to remain in the status quo, but your subconscious mind believes it will hurt more to change and that's why you stay stuck in damaging patterns. When you've been conditioned since childhood to fear rejection and abandonment like death, facing those realities will test your mettle. Cutting out the dead roots will create a new kind of pain, but it's one that has a purpose in helping you grow. In contrast, the torment you've experienced so far has likely only truncated your potential and kept you in that proverbial soggy container. Inside the toxic box, you prioritized managing unfulfilling relationships and circumstances at the expense of your connection with yourself.

With the tools in this book, you will access a new approach to life that does not depend on shiny new habits and strategies that only last until you lose the energy to police yourself. You do not have to forgive the people who hurt you or make excuses for them. Nor do you need to obsessively recite positive mantras or look on the bright side of things. The most important thing you can do is get honest with yourself and become curious about your thoughts, feelings, actions, and reactions rather than control them. Herein lies the difference between habit formation and transformation, which I hope sets this book apart from others on the topic of self-sabotage. When you stop trying to be a better person, stop arguing with yourself, and instead support yourself regardless of your thoughts and deeds, you will find healing.

Boundaries will become less of a strategy and more a natural consequence of the good feelings you have toward yourself. You will no longer tolerate the treatment you've been accepting all your life, not from a place of outrage, but of quiet acceptance that you deserve more. Rather than catching your thoughts and changing them, which is exhausting, you will accept them as they are. Aren't you tired of being hard on yourself, especially when it isn't getting you any closer to the life you desire? Even without self-admonishment, the healing journey is fraught with as many pitfalls as possibilities and there will be days when this work feels too hard. The alternative, however, ensures your demise, whether physical due to the mind-body connection or psychic because you denied your soul's calling (or even your most basic needs). If that sounds dire that's because it is. Like the plant with diseased roots rotting out its soil, time is of the essence for you to cut out what's killing you, so you can stay alive and thrive. Anaïs Nin put it more poetically when she said: "And the day came when the risk to remain tight in a bud was more painful than the risk it took to blossom."

One of the top regrets of people who are dying is that they wished they'd had the courage to live a life true to themselves, not the life others expected of them. It may feel easier to stay the same, but if this book has taught you anything, it's that avoiding discomfort in the short term only leads to agony down the line. Living inauthentically destroys your mental and physical health, taking years off your life and making the ones you have left feel like drudgery or worse. If another year, month, or day of living this way sounds intolerable to you, I urge you to begin taking the steps laid out in this book to prioritize your healing and put yourself first. That way, you will look back not with regret but with amazement and gratitude at how your life has transformed.

"When a flower doesn't bloom,
you fix the environment in which it grows,
not the flower."

ALEXANDER DEN HEIJER

NOTES

Introduction

Fraley, R. Chris. "A Brief Overview of Adult Attachment Theory and Research," n.d. http://labs.psychology.illinois.edu/~rcfraley/attachment.htm.

Chapter 1

Ham, Jacob. "Understanding Trauma: Learning Brain vs Survival Brain," July 25, 2017. https://www.youtube.com/watch?v=KoqaUANGvpA.

Zeltser, Francyne. "A Psychologist Shares the 4 Styles of Parenting—and the Type That Researchers Say Is the Most Successful." *CNBC*, July 1, 2021. https://www.cnbc.com/2021/06/29/child-psychology-explains-4-types-of-parenting-and-how-to-tell-which-is-right-for-you.html#:~:text=The%20four%20main%20parenting%20styles,Eleanor%20Maccoby%20and%20John%20Martin.

Pignatiello, Grant A., Richard J. Martin, and Ronald L. Hickman. "Decision Fatigue: A Conceptual Analysis." *Journal of Health Psychology.* U.S. National Library of Medicine, January 2020. https://www.ncbi.nlm.nih.gov/pmc/articles/PMC6119549/.

Danylchuk, Lisa. "What Do EMDR, Running, and Drumming Have in Common?" GoodTherapy.org Therapy Blog, January 6, 2020. https://www.goodtherapy.org/blog/what-do-emdr-running-and-drumming-have-in-common-0901154.

Chapter 2

Fraley, R. Chris. "A Brief Overview of Adult Attachment Theory and Research," n.d. http://labs.psychology.illinois.edu/~rcfraley/attachment.htm.

Levy, Terry. "Four Styles of Adult Attachment." Evergreen Psychotherapy Center, May 26, 2017. https://evergreenpsychotherapycenter.com/styles-adult-attachment/.

Team. "Avoidant Attachment Style: Causes and Adult Symptoms." Attachment Project, September 12, 2022. https://www.attachmentproject.com/blog/avoidant-attachment-style/.

Ray, Sefora Janel. "Five Ways to Help Anxious Attachment and Love More Securely." Therapytothrive.com, March 25, 2023. https://therapytothrive.com/2018/05/23/5-ways-to-help-anxious-attachment-and-love-more-securely/.

Team. "Disorganized Attachment Style: Everything You Need to Know." Attachment Project, September 12, 2022. https://www.attachmentproject.com/blog/disorganized-attachment/.

Hazan, Cindy, and Phillip Shaver. "Romantic Love Conceptualized as an Attachment Process." *Journal of Personality and Social Psychology* 52, no. 3 (1987): 511–24. https://doi.org/10.1037/0022-3514.52.3.511.

Brandon, Anna R., Sandra Pitts, Wayne H. Denton, C. Allen Stringer, and H. M. Evans. "A History of the Theory of Prenatal Attachment." *Journal of Prenatal & Perinatal Psychology & Health.* U.S. National Library of Medicine, 2009. https://www.ncbi.nlm.nih.gov/pmc/articles/PMC3083029/.

Chapter 3

"Are You the Family Scapegoat? Signs You May Be, and What You Can Do about It." ReGain, February 1, 2023. https://www.regain.us/advice/family/are-you-the-family-scapegoat-signs-you-may-be-and-what-you-can-do-about-it/.

Sherwood, Glynis. "12 Steps for Family Scapegoat Healing." October 4, 2022. https://glynissherwood.com/12-steps-for-family-scapegoat-healing/.

Aletta, Elvira G. "5 Steps to Stop Being the Family Scapegoat." *Explore What's Next,* December 30, 2019. https://www.explorewhatsnext.com/scapegoat/.

Chapter 4

Schumann, Karina, and Michael W Ross. "Why Women Apologize More Than Men." *Psychological Science* 21, no. 11 (September 20, 2010): 1649–55. https://doi.org/10.1177/0956797610384150.

Maté, Gabor. *When the Body Says No: The Cost of Hidden Stress.* London: Vermilion, 2019.

Getler, Al. "Dr. Henry Cloud—What Is Pruning?" YouTube, July 16, 2013. https://youtu.be/Q2tdjXc9F8k.

Chapter 5

Cloud, Henry, and John Sims Townsend. *Safe People: How to Find Relationships That Are Good for You and Avoid Those That Aren't.* Grand Rapids, MI: Zondervan, 2016.

Federal Bureau of Investigation. "Romance Scams," February 27, 2020. https://www.fbi.gov/news/stories/romance-scams.

Chapter 6

Wood, Joanne M., Wei Qi Elaine Perunovic, and John D. Lee. "Positive Self-Statements." *Psychological Science* 20, no. 7 (July 1, 2009): 860–66. https://doi.org/10.1111/j.1467-9280.2009.02370.x.

"Definition and Three Elements of Self-Compassion: Kristin Neff." July 9, 2020. https://self-compassion.org/the-three-elements-of-self-compassion-2/.

Lubit, Roy, Deborah Rovine, Lea Defrancisci, and Spencer Eth. "Impact of Trauma on Children." *Journal of Psychiatric Practice* 9, no. 2 (March 1, 2003): 128–38. https://doi.org/10.1097/00131746-200303000-00004.

Chapter 7

"Is Willpower a Limited Resource?—American Psychological Association." Accessed February 3, 2023. https://www.apa.org/topics/willpower-limited.pdf.

Brown, Brené. "Listening to Shame," n.d. https://www.ted.com/talks/brene_brown_listening_to_shame.

"Dr. Jonice Webb: Therapist, Author & Founder of CEN." Dr. Jonice Webb | Your resource for relationship and emotional health, November 1, 2022. https://drjonicewebb.com/.

Walker, Pete. "Vulnerable Self-Disclosure," n.d. http://pete-walker.com/pdf/vulnerable_self_disclosure.pdf.

Levine, Peter A. *Trauma and Memory: Brain and Body in a Search for the Living Past: A Practical Guide for Understanding and Working with Traumatic Memory.* Berkeley: North Atlantic, 2015.

Chapter 8

Szasz, Andrea. "Survivors of Childhood Trauma Often Grow Up Believing They Are Unworthy." *The Guardian*, January 29, 2023. https://www.theguardian.com/commentisfree/2023/jan/30/survivors-of-childhood-trauma-often-grow-up-believing-they-are-unworthy.

Center for Mindful Self-Compassion. "Center for Mindful Self-Compassion—Experience the Proven Power of Self-Compassion," July 28, 2022. https://centerformsc.org/.

Dreisoerner, Aljoscha, Nina M. Junker, Wolff Schlotz, Julia Heimrich, Svenja Bloemeke, Beate Ditzen, and Rolf van Dick. "Self-Soothing Touch and Being Hugged Reduce Cortisol Responses to Stress: A Randomized Controlled Trial on Stress, Physical Touch, and Social Identity." *Comprehensive Psychoneuroendocrinology* 8 (2021): 100091. https://doi.org/10.1016/j.cpnec.2021.100091.

"Mindfulness Exercise: Vagus Nerve Reset." YouTube, January 13, 2022. https://youtu.be/TONw4nCjb84.

Chapter 9

Lovering, Nancy. "The Link Between PTSD and Social Anxiety." Psych Central, August 17, 2022. https://psychcentral.com/ptsd/childhood-trauma-social-anxiety.

Pfaltz, Monique C., Sandra Passardi, Bianca Auschra, Natalia E. Fares-Otero, Ulrich Schnyder, and Peter Peyk. "Are You Angry at Me? Negative Interpretations of Neutral Facial Expressions Are Linked to Child Maltreatment but Not to Posttraumatic Stress Disorder." *European Journal of Psychotraumatology* 10, no. 1 (November 11, 2019). https://doi.org/10.1080/20008198.2019.1682929.

"The Evidence-Based Benefits of Loving-Kindness Meditation." Kripalu, October 9, 2019. https://kripalu.org/resources/evidence-based-benefits-loving-kindness-meditation.

Gordon, Amie M. "Think You Talk Too Much? New Research Suggests Otherwise." *Psychology Today*, September 27, 2022. https://www.psychologytoday.com/us/blog/between-you-and-me/202209/think-you-talk-too-much-new-research-suggests-otherwise.

Chapter 10

Peabody, Susan. *Addiction to Love: Overcoming Obsession and Dependency in Relationships.* Berkeley, CA: Celestial Arts, 2005.

Tanasugarn, Annie, PhD. "Overlaps Between Childhood Trauma and Adult Pathological Love." *Psychology Today*, March 13, 2023. https://www.psychologytoday.com/au/blog/understanding-ptsd/202211/

overlaps-between-childhood-trauma-and-adult-pathological-love.

PubMed. "The Compulsion to Repeat the Trauma. Re-Enactment, Revictimization, and Masochism," June 1, 1989. https://pubmed .ncbi.nlm.nih.gov/2664732.

Levine, Amir. *Attached.* London: Bluebird, 2019.

Chapter 11

Somer, Eli, Hisham M. Abu-Rayya, and Reut Brenner. "Childhood Trauma and Maladaptive Daydreaming: Fantasy Functions and Themes in a Multi-Country Sample." *Journal of Trauma & Dissociation* 22, no. 3 (May 27, 2021): 288–303. https://doi.org/10.1080/1 5299732.2020.1809599.

Maladaptive Daydreamer with Jayne Rachael. "Dr. Somer & Jayne Rachael Discuss Maladaptive Daydreaming, Recent Research, & MD Treatment Routes," January 30, 2022. https://www.youtube .com/watch?v=NTMMdSwrm7c.

Cleveland Clinic. "Maladaptive Daydreaming: What It Is, Symptoms & Treatment," n.d. https://my.clevelandclinic.org/health/ diseases/23336-maladaptive-daydreaming.

"APA PsycNet," n.d. https://psycnet.apa.org/record/2023-37728 -001.

Chapter 12

Center on the Developing Child at Harvard University. "What Are ACEs? and How Do They Relate to Toxic Stress?," October 30, 2020. https://developingchild.harvard.edu/resources/ aces-and-toxic-stress-frequently-asked-questions.

Esposito, Linda. "Learning to Parent Yourself as an Adult." *Psychology Today*, February 27, 2020. https://www.psychologytoday.com/ca/blog/anxiety-zen/201804/learning-parent-yourself-adult.

Toves, Anthony. "Take on the World by Re-Parenting Yourself." *Supportiv*, May 12, 2022. https://www.supportiv.com/healing/re-parenting-yourself.

Chapter 13

"Oprah's Favorite Definition of Forgiveness." Oprah.com, March 14, 2018. https://www.oprah.com/own-digitaloriginals/oprahs-favorite-definition-of-forgiveness-video.

"Tips for Writing a Coherent Narrative—Psychalive Ecourses." https://ecourse.psychalive.org/wp-content/uploads/2016/05/Coherent-Narrative.pdf.

Toussaint, Loren, Grant S. Shields, Gabriel Dorn, and George M. Slavich. "Effects of Lifetime Stress Exposure on Mental and Physical Health in Young Adulthood: How Stress Degrades and Forgiveness Protects Health." *Journal of Health Psychology* 21, no. 6 (June 1, 2016): 1004–14. https://doi.org/10.1177/1359105314544132.

Campbell, Joseph. *The Hero with a Thousand Faces.* Novato, CA: New World Library, 2008.

Chapter 14

University of California Television (UCTV). "A Cluttered Life: Middle-Class Abundance," October 30, 2013. https://www.youtube.com/watch?v=3AhSNsBs2Y0.

Goldman, Bruce. "How Men's and Women's Brains Are Different." *Stanford Medicine Magazine*, September 21, 2022. https://stanmed .stanford.edu/how-mens-and-womens-brains-are-different/.

Sears, Cori. "How to Identify and Treat Root Rot in Houseplants." *The Spruce*, July 20, 2022. https://www.thespruce.com/ treat-root-rot-houseplants-5223283.

Ware, Bronnie. *The Top Five Regrets of the Dying: A Life Transformed by the Dearly Departing.* Carlsbad, CA: Hay House, Inc., 2019.

ABOUT THE AUTHOR

LAURA K. CONNELL is a trauma-informed author and coach who helps clients uncover the hidden reasons they hold themselves back. She writes about healing self-sabotage and dysfunctional family dynamics at her website laurakconnell.com. Her articles have reached millions at *Life Hack, Pick the Brain, Dumb Little Man, Thought Catalog, Highly Sensitive Refuge, Chicken Soup for the Soul, The Globe and Mail, Toronto Star,* and more. Her popular online retreats and courses have helped thousands overcome the impact of toxic families. Born and raised in Toronto, Canada, she now makes her home in Tampa, Florida.